1966

Goethe, the Lyrist

UNIVERSITY OF NORTH CAROLINA
STUDIES IN THE GERMANIC LANGUAGES
AND LITERATURES

Publication Committee

FREDERIC E. COENEN, EDITOR

WERNER P. FRIEDERICH   GEORGE S. LANE

JOHN G. KUNSTMANN   HERBERT W. REICHERT

For other volumes in this series see page 183.

Foreign Sales through:
Librairie E. Droz
8 Rue Verdaine
Geneva, Switzerland

UNIVERSITY
OF NORTH CAROLINA
STUDIES IN
GERMANIC LANGUAGES
AND LITERATURES

———•———

NUMBER SIXTEEN

Goethe, the Lyrist

100 Poems in New Translations

facing the Originals

with a Biographical Introduction

by

EDWIN H. ZEYDEL

With an Appendix

on

Musical Settings to the Poems

Second Edition
Revised

THE UNIVERSITY OF NORTH CAROLINA PRESS

CHAPEL HILL

To

BAYARD QUINCY MORGAN

Translator, Teacher, Critic

In Gratitude

Contents

Preface

In her monograph, *Goethe's Lyric Poems in English Translation Prior to 1860,* published in the University of Wisconsin Studies (No. 6) in 1919, Lucretia Van Tuyl Simmons writes (page 78) : "As the author of *Faust* and of other dramas, as the author of novels, tales, autobiography, and letters, we are able to draw very near to Goethe, in English translations. Any one of the standard sets of Goethe's complete works will convey to us a fairly accurate knowledge of his genius, in all fields *except the lyric*; here he is still *terra incognita,*—or worse." And yet her careful study and the monograph of Stella Hinz (No. 26 in the same series, published in 1928), which carries the investigation to 1924, show that some four thousand attempts were made up to that date to translate separate poems, a few essayed dozens of times. And among the translators are found such names as Thomas and Jane Carlyle, Samuel Taylor Coleridge, Sir Walter Scott, Percy Bysshe Shelley, Henry Wadsworth Longfellow, William Cullen Bryant, John Greenleaf Whittier, Harriet Beecher Stowe, and Edward McDowell.

What may be the reason why, with the exception of a mere handful, such as Longfellow's renderings of the two Wanderer's Night Songs, none of these translations has taken root in English or American soil, while of the dozen or more translations of the complete *Faust,* at least three or four are acceptable? Those who believe that poetry, especially lyric poetry, defies translation will derive enough reason from that belief. The studies of Miss Simmons and Miss Hinz give the answer to others. Many of the translators were too foreign to the world and thought of Goethe. Some had an imperfect command of his language. Most of them, missing the simplicity and directness of the German poet, strove to compose poems that were pretty, but lost the meaning, or spirit, or both, of one of the world's greatest lyrists. Many, even of the best, used a stilted idiom which the reader of today, familiar with Frost, Robinson, and Sandburg, can no longer relish. The *Faust* translators, on the other hand, in some cases at least, were better qualified and worked with more care.

There is no such comprehensive study of the translations since 1924 as exists for the earlier period. However, since two world-wide Goethe celebrations have taken place during the interim, the centennial of his death in 1932 and the bicentennial of his birth in 1949, we would have a right to expect numerous modern translations. But this expectation has not been fulfilled. The most important new renderings have appeared in a volume, *The Permanent Goethe,* for which Thomas Mann claims editorial responsibility (New York, Dial Press, second printing, 1953). It contains 47 shorter poems and eight pages of epigrams and sayings in verse. But over one-half of these translations are old standbys of Bowring, Martin, Aytoun, Dwight, Drysen, and other nineteenth century translators, many of them long ago discredited by critics. The new renderings are by Stephen Spender (10), Isidor Schneider (epigrams), F. Melian Stawell (7), and Nora P. Wydenbruck, a collaborator of Stawell. Though done in a modern idiom, they are not faithful in spirit or form to the originals. Good poems though they may be, they are not good translations.

The Permanent Goethe, however, suffers not only from poor choice of translations, it is also not edited consistently well. Thus, on page xxxviii Goethe's famous "Willkommen und Abschied" is called "Welcome and Farewell," with one stanza quoted in translation, while on page 10 the same poem is named "Greeting and Departure" and given in a quite different rendering. The same curious treatment is accorded the aphorism on America (pages xliii and 655).

Better translations of shorter poems of Goethe than these have been made since 1924, but they have, to my knowledge, not appeared in print in any appreciable numbers. In the library of Stanford University there is a bound typescript, *A Book of Goethe's Verse,* by Bayard Quincy Morgan (1937), containing about 130 renderings, the majority of them new, but some revised and two unchanged from older translations. Morgan, familiar with thousands of older versions, had at first planned to compile an eclectic collection, such as was suggested by Miss Simmons, but soon found this to be unfeasible and set to work making new translations, with the help here and there of some good lines or suitable rhymes of a predecessor. But Morgan admits that he has at times fallen short of his aim.

If after the passage of a generation criticism of his work is still appropriate, I would praise his almost too faithful adherence to meaning, rhyme scheme, rhythm, and melody, but regret his loss of Goethe's natural simplicity and naive spontaneity of language, and his tendency to use a type of poetic diction quite foreign to the spirit of Goethe. Such expressions as "it fills me with amaze," "as he lists," "knewst thou," "wilt, lovely boy, thou with me abide?," "a youth did wend him," "I'll prick thee so, thou'lt remember me for woe," "when the moon I gaze" and countless others are reminiscent enough of older English poetical tradition, but convey a false impression when applied to Goethe.

Recently I saw a collection of about one hundred new translations, still unpublished, by Joseph S. Height of Wabash College, Indiana. Since they were still in a process of refinement, it would be unfair to express more than the hope that they may be published some day. Height lays special emphasis upon simplicity, spontaneity, and plasticity of expression and studiously avoids all stilted "poetic" language. But the virtue of Morgan's work—meticulous attention to Goethe's rhythm and melody—was still to be achieved by Height when I saw the manuscript.

The renderings of some one hundred poems of Goethe included in the present volume are based upon principles of translation which should be set forth at the outset. They are criteria and standards which in my opinion should guide any translator and his critics.

That the standards of today are different from those still observed by Pope in the eighteenth century is generally conceded. The true translator must above all strive for completeness and accuracy both in substance and in form. The entire subject matter in its fullest extent, with careful attention to shades of meaning, connotations, and imagery, must be envisaged—nothing more or less. There is no such thing as "translator's license," except perhaps for a genius. On the other hand, mere dictionary faithfulness would be just as fatal. As to form, which is often best caught unconsciously, all the stylistic qualities—word choice, sentence arrangement, mood, meter, cadence, rhythm, and melody—must be intelligently apprehended and skillfully conveyed in a first-class rendering.

It would not do to subscribe to the theory that translations, especially of metrical works, need not be made in the spirit of the original, and that rhythm and style, for instance, may be transmuted to the spirit of the translator's age, as was done by Pope in his Homer. Nor do prose translations of poetry fully carry out the purpose of a real translation because they can reproduce only one phase of it—substance. The history of Shakespeare's reception in Germany furnishes the best illustration of the limits of a prose rendering as compared with one that takes form and spirit into account. The Eschenburg prose translations, which appeared between 1775 and 1782, served only to inspire the critics to study Shakespeare and the poets to read him in English, while the poetical renderings of A. W. Schlegel, begun less than a generation later, all but made Shakespeare a German poet in the eyes of the German people.

In the case of Goethe's shorter poems, care must also be taken to preserve that simplicity, crystalline clarity, and total absence of preciosity and affectation of which I have spoken. I have therefore striven to prefer the homely, everyday word, to restrict the use of the archaic "thou" and "thee," and in general to give the poems the Goethean ring of genuineness which makes them still readable and enjoyable in the original.

I have also taken pains throughout to adhere to the meters and rhyme schemes of Goethe, including the feminine rhymes and endings which too many predecessors have ignored but which German poetry and Goethe in particular cultivate with success. When these are replaced by masculine rhymes and endings, Goethe's poems, especially the pure lyrics and ballads, suffer markedly. However, in English care must be taken to avoid too many feminine rhymes of the same type, such as -ing rhymes. They easily mislead the translator into an awkward un-English style. In some cases, therefore, the translations substitute masculine for feminine rhymes, but since the German originals are under the reader's eye, this should be no obstacle to the appreciation of the swing of Goethe's poems. In IX, 22, I have overcome the lack of feminine rhymes in ll. 1-3 by compensation in ll. 2-4. Yet, everything considered, I agree with what Goethe says in his epigram on thought *versus* rhyme (IX, 10), and have been guided accordingly.

Although all the renderings, with the possible exception of IV, 11 are my own, I have not hesitated to take over an occasional rhyme, or even an entire line, or several lines, from my predecessors. More often, though, these lines too have been revised or polished. Among those to whom I am consciously indebted to this extent are: Oxenford (III, 5), Dwight (III, 6; IV, 1), Longfellow (IV, 11-12), Bayard Taylor (VI, 6; IX, 22), Carlyle (VI, 7), Bancroft (VI, 8), Merivale (VI, 10), Bowring (VI, 4, 11, 12; VIII, 7), and Martin (VI, 12). To Bayard Quincy Morgan, to whom this volume is dedicated, I am more deeply indebted (e.g. III, 6; IV, 1; VI, 12, 21; VIII, 10; IX, 1). His careful fidelity to *form* may serve as a model for all future translators. When I saw Joseph S. Height's renderings, mine were already well on the way to completion, and a few had been published. But the care with which he reproduces the plain, sincere *spirit* of Goethe's *language* must be an inspiration to any translator who would meet the poet on his own level.

Longfellow's renderings of the two Wanderer's Night Songs (IV, 11 and 12) are probably the best of any thus far attempted in English. If I have tried my hand at these poems again, I was not prompted by any ridiculous desire to improve upon Longfellow as a poet, but I aimed to get a little closer to Goethe. In IV, 11, I could do no better than follow Longfellow in all but several lines. These are in part influenced by, though not copied from, Morgan, but in the last line, in which both lose the key word *süsser*, I have tried to make good the deficiency. My new try at IV, 12, which has probably been attempted by more translators than any other Goethe poem, represents an effort to recapture the lilt. Where Longfellow missed the feminine rhymes throughout the poem, and lost the majesty of *Ist Ruh* in line 2, I have tried to restore the poem at least to its original mould.

It would be a mistake to ignore the numerous musical compositions—now almost three thousand in number—which Goethe's shorter poems have inspired. I have tried out many of my renderings against the best-known of these, and in the Appendix, which is partly indebted to *Die Lese der deutschen Lyrik* of Friedrich Bruns, (New York, 1938), give more information on the subject than has ever before been given in English.

Throughout this volume the translations are brought face to face with Goethe's originals, since it is my conviction that this is the best way of presenting poems in translation, even for readers who may have only the barest knowledge of the original language. In judging the poems themselves, it should be remembered that they were written between approximately 1770 and 1830, and that styles have changed in poetry, as in almost everything else, though not always for the better. The poems should, therefore, be approached in a historical spirit, as expressions of their age.

As for choice of poems, I have striven to include the most popular ones. If my translations find favor, I should be glad later to attempt another collection of those for the omission of which I may now be taken to task.

The Biographical Introduction is intended to be only a sketchy account of Goethe's development as a poet in the fields which his shorter poems represent, and not a biography as such. It is suggested that since the Introduction presents a running commentary on the poems, it be read concurrently with the poems. It is indebted to many sources, particularly to the edition of Goethe's poems by Clarence Willis Eastman (New York, 1941).

Much has been made in the Introduction of what some critics term the poet's *standards of intent,* which explain the genesis of an art work on biographical bases. But it should be realized that there are at least two other interactive types of standards for interpreting poetry, *viz.* those of *correspondence* (the stringencies of subject matter) and those of *coherence* (the interrelations of the elements of the interpretations, or an interpretation of a particular part of the work tested by its coherence with the rest of its parts).[1] To Goethe's poems, too, all three standards should be applied, although limited space permitted only partial treatment in this volume.

Although a full account of Goethe as a lyrist (in the broader sense) has not yet appeared either in German or in English, two English books besides Eastman's edition can be especially recommended: Barker Fairley's *Goethe as Revealed in his Poetry* (Chicago, 1932) and August Closs's *The Genius of the German Lyric* (London, 1938, pp. 230-244; 272-279). The most recent anthology of Goethe's selected poems for study in the original

---

[1] See Abraham Kaplan and Ernest Kris in *Philosophy and Phenomenological Research* VIII, 3, and Isabel C. Hungerland in *The Journal of Aesthetics and Art Criticism* XIII, 3.

by English-speaking readers is by Barker Fairley (New York, 1955).

The task of capturing Goethe's shorter poems in English will probably never be completed. All I would say of my efforts is that they are directed toward a better understanding and appreciation of these poems on the part of English-speaking readers today.

I express sincere thanks to Professor Victor Lange of Cornell University for very helpful criticism of parts of the manuscript, and to the Charles Phelps Taft Memorial Fund of the University of Cincinnati for financing this volume, also to Professor Frederic E. Coenen, general editor of this series, for his interest and help.

Introduction

GOETHE'S DEVELOPMENT AS A LYRIST

If it may be said that the function of the poet is to cast a rhythmic spell through imaginative language for the purpose of freeing, magnifying, and uplifting man's spirit, then Goethe achieves that function as well as few others have. In his poetry this rhythmic spell is magically woven by "words that have become deeds" (to use Robert Frost's phrase), generalized human experiences, usually of the poet himself. For Goethe is one of the world's most subjective writers. Although much of his poetry is enshrined in his dramas (*Faust, Iphigenia at Tauris, Torquato Tasso*) and narrative poems (*Hermann and Dorothea*), yet it finds its simplest and most delightful expression in his lyrics and ballads.

A few of his German predecessors in the eighteenth century, Klopstock, Günther, and Claudius, had been groping to achieve a lyric poetry of personal experience, but it was not before the early "Storm and Stress" period of Goethe in the seventeen-seventies that this goal was attained in Germany. From that time on, German poetry possesses, in its greatest lyrists, the qualities which Goethe gave it—the power of expressing profound experiences of an outstanding personality, and of revealing his inmost being, so that the gap between life and its articulation in poetry is closed.

Almost from the beginning Goethe knew the secret that the lyrist must start with a concrete object, and not an abstraction, and in contemplation of it must develop the core idea. Then, in the seventies, when the recording of his experiences became an inner necessity, and his poems welled forth of their own accord, as a rule from the mood that these experiences had engendered, carrying their own rhythms to his ear, he attained greatness as a lyrist. "Es sang in mir," he said; he was constrained to be the poet. This poetry became a sort of lay confessional that gave him surcease from sorrow and confirmation of joy, but impressed the reader with a feeling that all this was more than personal, was universal human experience.

But Goethe and his poetry did not spring from the brow of Zeus, and the dictum of Archibald MacLeish that "a poem should not mean, but be" did not become immediately apparent in his work. That warmheartedness, sharp vision, and many-sided contact with life which later were opened to him, and that perfect control of language and its music which he acquired, came only with maturation. So too his ability for finding the symbol of what is eternal in the world of material things.

Johann Wolfgang Goethe (the *von* of nobility was not acquired until 1782), born on August 28, 1749, in the free imperial city of Frankfort on the Main, was the son of a stern jurist of some wealth and considerable education and culture who in his thirties had married a charming young girl of seventeen with a cheerful, ebullient poetic disposition. It was from her that the eldest born inherited his happy temperament (**IX, 11**).* Together with his sister Cornelia, less than two years his junior, he received practically all his early education at home at the hands of his father and private tutors. In 1765, at the age of sixteen, he was ready for higher education. Sent to the University of Leipzig to study law, he devoted himself also to literature and extra-curricular activities which acquainted him with life and made a man of him. During these three Leipzig years the poet in him was awakened, too. His acquaintance with Kätchen Schönkopf, an innkeeper's daughter, whom he calls Annette in some of his earlier poems, with the artist and sculptor Oeser and his daughter Friederike, had more than a passing influence upon him.

Chapter I.

The two poems of our opening chapter **I** are not from the collection called *Annette,* but from the New Songs (*Neue Lieder*), twenty poems set to music by Bernhard Theodor Breitkopf, a scion of the famous family which founded the publishing firm later known as Breitkopf and Härtel, and which also published these *Neue Lieder* (dated 1770 but actually got out in 1769). These poems still reveal signs of immaturity, are written in the frivolous rococo style of the period, and betray the impact of the writer Wieland. **I,** 2 was written with memories of Kätchen, and the Anacreontic motif of inconstancy is clearly in the foreground. But it should be realized that already at this early stage—Goethe was not yet twenty—his images are concrete (e.g. the dragon fly in **I,** 1), not abstract, and that he develops a core idea on this basis. His keen observation of nature,

---

* This and subsequent symbols refer to our collection of poems.

too, is noteworthy. Moreover, the verses are smooth and elegant—worthy of an Alexander Pope. These are signs that the remarkable development of his lyric art that was to follow soon had already begun in embryonic fashion.

Chapter II

As August Closs notes in his chapter on Goethe in "Die neuere deutsche Lyrik" (*Deutsche Philologie im Aufriss*) cols. 63f., the period of long recuperation at home (1768-1770) after the Leipzig interlude, intensified the young poet's inner life under the influence of his mother's Pietist friend, Susanna Katharina von Klettenberg (born 1723). This helped prepare him for the experiences of his second university period in Strassburg (1770-1771) and of his love for Friederike, the daughter of the country vicar J. J. Brion in the nearby village of Sesenheim. If to this we add his keener sensitivity to nature; the profound impression of the Gothic cathedral in Strassburg, then erroneously considered a typical example of German medieval art; the influence of Hamann, the East Prussian philosopher, who taught that a poet is a demoniac creator; and of Herder, the theologian-philosopher, who directed him to the Middle Ages and the Renaissance, to poetry as the mother-tongue of mankind, and to the Bible, Homer, Ossian, Shakespeare, and the folk poetry of all nations—then we have the main factors that explain the young poet of 1770-1771.

Of all these influences that of Herder was probably the most potent at the time. In later life, particularly in his dramas (*Iphigenia, Torquato Tasso,* and *Faust II*) and in *Hermann and Dorothea,* Goethe turned strongly to classical antiquity for inspiration. In his lyrical poetry, however, where his interests, though not forgetful of the ancient classics, are more comprehensive and in general more folk-bound, he stayed much closer to Herder.

The Sesenheim experience is important enough in Goethe's life and lyricism to merit a separate chapter, although even at this time he has not fully freed himself from conventionalism. The experience lasted from October, 1770, to next August. In retrospect Goethe told the story of this romantic episode of his life over forty years later in his autobiography, *Poetry and Truth (Dichtung und Wahrheit),* Books X and XI, touching up the story with some dashes of "poetry." No doubt his love for this natural, unspoiled girl, the spirit of which has been well caught by Franz Lehar in the operetta *Friederike*, was the most compelling and elemental he had yet experienced.

We have no external evidence to identify **II, 1**, with Sesenheim, yet there is no doubt that it belongs to the Sesenheim group, even though Goethe did not publish it until 1775. In it "Storm and Stress" in all its power erupts with pantheistic feeling. Not an event, but a condition is described, a condition completely identified with the poet. Here we truly have a poem that does not mean, but is, and words that have become deeds. Never before in literature had nature and love poetry been so perfectly fused as in this ecstatic outcry of joy by a poet drunk at the same time with love and with nature bursting forth in Maytime splendor. **II, 2**, perhaps the most famous of all Goethe's poems, shows him strongly under the influence of the folk song and of his mentor, Herder. A crude folk poem with a very similar refrain had already appeared early in the seventeenth century, and in 1774 Herder published another variant from memory. Goethe's version, bearing the stamp of his own personality, and with Friederike and himself as the girl and boy, was not printed until 1789.

3 and 4 once again show the Anacreontic influence and the playful spirit of the rococo age, yet they are to be rated much higher than the average product of that period of pose and artificiality. Concerning 3, Goethe tells us in *Poetry and Truth* that at that time painted ribbons had just become the style; he painted several and sent them to Friederike with these lines. This poem is now sung in Switzerland and various parts of Germany in several corrupted versions. Blind man's buff (4) was a favorite pastime among the younger set. Goethe was still fond of such fictitious names as Theresa, typical of the pastoral style. The pregnant language, in line 12, for instance: "You coldly set the blind man free," for "you coldly set me free, whereupon I was immediately blindfolded," is characteristic of Goethe.

5, with its striking imagery, reminiscent of Shakespeare, is a poem of higher merit. Its rhythm, too, is well suited to the situation and mood. Although some of the images may have been suggested during a night ride into the mountains of Lorraine, Goethe actually used to travel from Strassburg to Sesenheim on horseback. As it now stands, the poem might be interpreted as his farewell from Friederike.

Chapter III

Goethe's return to Frankfort saw the execution of his plan to dramatize the life of Götz von Berlichingen, an unconventional attempt to resuscitate the memory of the valiant old robber baron and feuder of Martin Luther's days. Written in the spirit of Shakespeare as Goethe then understood him, it is typical of the young poet and typical of the age of "Storm and Stress" which he ushered in with this play—an age that under Rousseau's influence threw all authority, all "dead learning" to the winds and worshipped the intuitive, imaginative, and emotional side of man. Only the individualist, the "original genius," was tolerated. Sir Walter Scott translated it in 1799.

During the next four years other new experiences crowded in upon young Goethe: his stay in Wetzlar (May to September, 1772), where he, now licensed to practice law, was sent by his father to study the workings of the hopelessly cumbersome Cameral Court of the moribund Holy Roman Empire, but where, too, he had an unhappy love affair with a betrothed girl, Charlotte Buff, which led to the writing of the short but emotionally powerful sentimental novel, *The Sorrows of Young Werther* (1774); and his none too happy years at home (1772-1775), where he finally broke off his engagement with his beloved Lili Schönemann. These experiences helped turn him ever farther away from conventional barriers of poetry. His powers as a creative lyrist grew apace during these early "Storm and Stress" years.

III, 1, 2, 3 are thoroughly characteristic of young Goethe at this time. He has burst the bonds of traditional prosody and uses free verse, as he does also in *Faust I,* and the *Urfaust* (or earlier version), when Faust summons the Earth Spirit. Coachman Cronos (1), the father of Zeus, is pictured driving Goethe through life in his stagecoach. The ride has its moments of "nauseous dizziness," and the road is rough, but life must be lived out to the full, and all its joys, including those offered by a maiden at her threshold, must be tasted. While life may be brutal, it is not to be shunned as evil. In the end he urges more speed, lest he be overtaken by senility "with tottering frame" and "jaws that are toothless." His defiant pagan attitude toward death makes him bid the driver announce their coming proudly to Orcus, the Lower World, that so important a personage as the poet may be graciously greeted.

A spirit no less defiant is expressed in 2, where Zeus, who had banished Prometheus to earth for the theft of fire, is warned that the gods are dependent, in their turn, on man, and that even they are subject to fate. Prometheus, as the creator of man, has found the gods unbending and cruel, and now he sneers at them, as they had at him. Man, the creation of Prometheus, can stand proudly on his own feet and spite the smug, impervious gods. It was probably Herder who had called Goethe's attention to Prometheus, an idol of "Storm and Stress." The material of this poem was originally intended by Goethe for a drama in the style of the *Urfaust* (which he took along to Weimar in 1775).

In 3 Goethe uses the myth of Ganymede, the most beautiful of mortals who was snatched up to Olympus to be the cupbearer of Zeus. This symbol serves him as the vehicle for those feelings which come over him as he observes the budding and striving of spring. Here the love element, coupled so effectively with the nature motif in the earlier "Song of May" (II, 1), is less obtrusive, though the poem breathes the spirit of the early pages of *The Sorrows of Young Werther*. We cannot help but notice, however, how much firmer Goethe's grip on his art has become. What were once mere decorative "young gods with springtime powers" (II, 3) have now become meaningful symbols of man's relation to higher beings. That all the free-verse poems of the type of 1-3 were not couched in terms of classical mythology, is shown by "Mahomet's Song," not included in our collection.

All the rest of the poems in Chapter III, except 12, bear some relationship to Lili Schönemann, who was but seventeen when Goethe became engaged to her in April of 1775. She was not only attractive, but sensible, witty, a little coquettish, and possessed of social graces. She drew Goethe into a lively social whirl, and he spent some happy-unhappy months in her company. 4 and 5 were both written about two months before the engagement. The name Belinda of 4 is reminiscent of conventional Anacreontic nomenclature, while the gaming places and unbearable grimaces refer to his activities in Lili's company and to her relatives and friends. 5 alludes again to his quandary.

He loves her dearly, yet his sense of loyalty to himself bids him desist. Nevertheless the engagement took place. In May, however, he broke away for two months—as he often did when a situation got out of control—, journeying to Switzerland with the two Counts Stolberg, to test his feelings for her. 6, written on Lake Zurich in June, shows that he has not forgotten her; even the meter changes as his thoughts turn to her in line 9. Only when the skiff finally approaches land, does the poet's mood become calmer, and we have a foreboding how the engagement is bound to end. 7, composed on the same day, as the party ascended the hill overlooking the lake, again clearly reveals his distraction.

8 must have been penned just before the final separation from Lili in September. To explain the "twin-born clusters" in line 5, we may refer to an observation in Goethe's botanical notes that in the grape the ovary develops from two leaves. In 9 and 10 the engagement with Lili has been broken; Goethe has turned his back on Frankfurt and gone to Weimar. 11 is also a product of the early Weimar days and still refers to Lili. The wound continues to smart.

It is idle to say that perhaps Goethe should have married Lili. Too many obstacles seem to have stood in their way. He dreaded his own fickleness, but also his loss of freedom. He felt he was not ready for marriage—and indeed we may wonder whether he ever was. Lili's friends, as well as the two families, were opposed. And yet, years later Goethe confessed to the world that she was the first and only real love he ever had. His drama *Stella*, written during this time, idealizes her. Poem 10 was sent to her with a copy of the play. 12, written in 1774, epigrammatically expresses Goethe's contempt for reviewers and critics.

Chapter IV

It was in early November of 1775 that Goethe, accepting an invitation of the young ruler, Duke Karl August (born 1758), who had just assumed the reins of government in his tiny principality, went to Weimar on what was expected to be a visit. He remained, with interruptions, for the rest of his life, acting in the early years as a mentor to the prince and exercising a moderating influence upon the ebullient youth. In the course of the years Goethe held such positions as privy councilor of legation, privy councilor, president of the chamber of finance, commissioner of war and highways, and director of the court theatre and of the scientific institutes of the University of Jena. Of literary projects he brought along from Frankfort both the *Urfaust* and *Egmont*, a lyrical drama on the fate of Count Egmont, a martyr of the Dutch struggle for independence in the sixteenth century (finished in 1787).

Although Lili could not so soon be forgotten, Goethe was before long drawn into the orbit of another woman, Madame Charlotte von Stein. Seven years his senior, she was a lady of literary culture, once a lady-in-waiting at the court, now the wife of the duke's equerry, and the mother of seven children. His love for her soon grew sincere and deep, as his many notes and letters to her attest. But here, at least, he could feel safe so far as marriage was concerned. IV, 1, written in the little town of Ilmenau, near Weimar, in 1776, was inspired by his first strong passion for her, who gradually became his confidante. The thought that joys can be just as painful as sorrows and often go hand in hand with them, is a commonplace with this poet. IV, 2, was sent to her as a letter in 1776. Besides being a poem of high merit, it is a most revealing document, showing how much Charlotte meant to him. In some far-removed past, he feels, in another life, they had known and loved each other. Stanza 4, often misunderstood, does not, however, refer to their actual relationship, but to the imagined one "in some past generation." The hopelessness of the situation is a keynote of the poem, which was not published until 1848. 3 refers to the house and garden in the valley of the Ilm river on the outskirts of Weimar (known as the "Gartenhaus"), which the duke presented to Goethe in 1776.

The next three poems (4-6) are again written in free verse. 4 is reminiscent of Goethe's second journey to Switzerland, where at Lauterbrunnen he saw the Staubbach, a slender thread of water falling about a thousand feet and vaporized before it empties into the Lütschine river, which later flows into placid Lake Brienz. This symbolic poem was conceived as an antiphonal song, with two spirits singing alternately. 5, probably written in 1781, might be considered a counterpart to "Prometheus Speaks" (III, 2); now the poet's defiance has been softened to a more humble outlook upon life. No doubt Charlotte had much to do with this change. Then, too, under the impact of

affairs of state and the sobering opposition of some of the
duke's older councilors, who objected to the admission of young
Goethe (not even of noble birth!) to the higher councils of gov-
ernment, Goethe's period of "Storm and Stress" was nearing an
end and making way for clarification. 6 was written in 1783
and asserts man's kinship with the Divine Being. Not negative
protest against the "changeless iron-bound statutes" of nature,
but the positive conviction that the achievements of man's
creative spirit have durability, marks this poem. Going beyond
what he had said in 5, Goethe here emphasizes the lasting quality
of man's spiritual powers.

7, much of which is in the form of a dialog between the god-
dess of truth and the poet, was written in 1784 on a journey to
the Harz mountains and placed at the head of his collected
works, which appeared in 1787-1790. The opening of the poem
was inspired by the mist over the valley of the Saale river near
Jena, gradually dissipated by the rising sun. In the figure of
the goddess of truth we can again discern Charlotte, whom a
few months later he addressed as "you dear guide of my soul."
As a poet, Goethe intimates, he is the solitary high priest of
truth, but truth can only be seen and enjoyed by mortals
through a gauze veil of poetry. As in *Faust*, renunciation is
preached, and man's ambition to play the superman is derided.
Line 70 refers to the parable in Matthew 25, 15 ff.

8, now generally considered one of Goethe's maturest and
finest poems, was in its original version of 1777 (revised ten
years later) a very personal asseveration of love, meant only
for Charlotte. When he left her for Italy in 1786, she wrote a
bitter parody of it. In its present form, though conceived to
assuage Charlotte, it is depersonalized and has universal ap-
peal. But its full meaning is difficult to grasp without some
help.

In an article devoted to the poem (in *The German Quarterly*
XXVI, 1), Harold Jantz offers a clear, acceptable interpreta-
tion. "The main theme," he says, "is loneliness finding its way
back to friendship. The moon dominates the first three stanzas,
the stream the next four, and the envisioned friend the last
two. The first part has recollections of time past, the second
leads out of the past through the present and on to the future,
which is the concern of the third part." The first two stanzas,
spoken to the moon, deal with the healing magic of the moon-lit

night. In the third, the moon, the distant friend, beams into the poet's soul and brings him recollection of sad and joyful days, which extend over into his present loneliness. The transition to stanza 4 and what follows, dominated by the stream, is achieved through the reference to loneliness at the end of stanza 3. The poet feels desolate; friendship is gone (stanza 4). In stanza 5 the "bitter paradox" that "the past still lingers with him in ever-present memory" saddens him. Stanzas 6 and 7 belong together, and "the implication of remorseless dissipation by time" is relieved by "the call to ceaseless forward motion in time." The cycle of the seasons leads over into the future. Even winter cannot arrest the stream, and it gives way to spring. As the stream goes on irresistibly, so does man. After chilling desolation, the warm spring of love and friendship follows. "The two new-found friends in nature, the moon and the stream, lead the poet once more to the hope and expectation of renewed human friendship." Thus the tragic experiences of the past leave no bitter feelings—only the wisdom of resignation, and "the images of friendship increase in closeness."

Among all the verbal beauties—Jantz refers especially to "the union of inner and outer music" in stanzas 6 and 7—note also the effect of the many liquid sounds in the early stanzas, in describing the limpid moonlight.

9 was printed for the first time in 1776, but in later editions included in a collection entitled "Art." Though not published until 1789, 10 is at least five years older, and may even go back to the sentimental days of *The Sorrows of Young Werther*. The world, says Goethe, is drearier when man's tears are checked than when they flow freely. 11 was written early in 1776 and sent to Charlotte late that year. It has sometimes been given a specifically Christian interpretation and in an altered form has entered hymnologies. Like 12, it is known in America through Longfellow's translation. Here again joy and grief are thought of as complementary, as complementary as they are in the *Lay of the Nibelungs*. Not until the seventh line is "Sweet Peace" mentioned; the prayer itself then embraces only six words. 12 dates from the late summer of 1780 and was scribbled by Goethe on the wooden wall of a small hunting lodge near the summit of Gickelhahn hill above the town of Ilmenau, facing the setting sun. Over fifty years later, and less than seven months before his death, Goethe revisited the spot and

read his lines again with deep emotion. In 1870 the lodge burned down, and an exact replica was built; a photograph of the poem hangs on the wall. The musical expression of the emotion which pervades it, with the perfect repose of line 2 and the promise, at the end, not of inexorable death, but of rest, is achieved by a wealth of euphony, assonance, and rhyme which is matchless. **13** was written in 1785 and intended possibly for inclusion in a vaudeville which Goethe never finished. Was the poet perhaps harking back to Lili?

Chapter V

Even before leaving Frankfort in 1775, Goethe had probably begun work on a markedly autobiographical novel, the first version of which, completed in 1785 (but not published in this form until 1911), bore the title *Wilhelm Meister's Theatrical Mission* (*Wilhelm Meisters theatralische Sendung*). In 1795-1796 it was thoroughly revised and expanded and published as *Wilhelm Meister's Apprenticeship* (*Wilhelm Meisters Lehrjahre*), with a much broader mission set for its hero—apprenticeship for life. It is from this novel that the four songs in Chapter V are taken.

1, written in 1783 or 1784, is sung by one of the principal characters, Mignon, a tragic, mysterious figure. When the hero meets her, she is attached to a company of itinerant circus folk and being maltreated by her master. Wilhelm becomes her protector and guardian by buying her freedom. She grows to love him, and when he has an amour with another woman, Mignon dies of a broken heart. In the original version of the poem, she calls him "master" (*Gebieter*) in the last line of each stanza. The poem offers us three phases of her vague childhood recollections: of the country and landscape, of a palace in which she was reared, and of the Alpine passes leading north from Italy, whence she had come. These last memories are Goethe's, too. On the journey to Switzerland in 1775 he had travelled on foot to the summit of the St. Gotthard pass. The poem idealizes Goethe's yearning, which was then and still is the yearning of many Germans, for the sunny skies and land of Italy. It is the basis for Mignon's song "Connais-tu le pays?" in Ambroise Thomas' opera *Mignon* (1866), dependent in a general way upon Goethe's novel.

2 is sung by Mignon to an accompaniment by the Harper,

but expresses the yearning of Wilhelm for a fair Amazon, who had saved his life. In 1785 Goethe sent the poem to Charlotte von Stein in a letter. His own longing is also enshrined in it. 3 and 4, probably two years older, are sung by this Harper, a half-mad graybeard who travels with Wilhelm and Mignon and who, it turns out, is really the high-born father of Mignon by his own sister, whom he had married without realizing her identity.

Chapter VI

The arrangement of the poems in Chapters I-V has been roughly chronological, but those in VI do not follow such a sequence. 1, first printed in 1815 in the new edition of Goethe's works in twenty volumes (1815-1819), immediately after the "Dedication" (IV, 7), is a fitting prelude to our chapter because it is meant as an apology for offering a motley array of poems penned at different times and in divergent moods.

2, first printed in 1800, served as an introduction after "Dedication" in the edition of the works published 1806-1810. Then, in the edition of 1815-1819, it was assigned a place after 1. Here, as later in *Poetry and Truth*, Goethe intimates that his writings are "fragments of a great confession." In the poem he adds that such confession is better in verse than in prose.

3-12 introduce a series of some of Goethe's most famous ballads, interrupted for variety only by 4 (a song of Clärchen, the heroine of the drama *Egmont*) and 6 (sung in *Faust* by Margaret at the spinning wheel, when her mood vacillates between shame and sorrow, and yearning and passion). 3 appeared in 1775 in a melodrama, and may be considered a foil to "Rose in the Heather" (II, 2), though it is less virile and perhaps too sweetly Anacreontic. But here it is the girl who is the aggressor. 5, composed as early as 1773-1774, was already in the *Urfaust*—the first song sung by Margaret after being accosted by Faust. The goblet symbolizes an undying love that cannot be handed down to others. Thule, according to the Greek navigator Pytheas of the fourth century B.C., was the northernmost land beyond Britain, where the sun sets.

7 first appeared in *Wilhelm Meister's Apprenticeship*. Stanzas 2, 4, 5 and most of 6 are spoken by the minstrel. For the poet, Goethe avers, poetry is its own reward. 8, first printed in 1779, expresses the mysterious attraction which bodies of

water had for him. His first glimpse of the sea, however, did not come until 1786, when he visited Venice. The mood of the poem is said to have been called forth by the suicide, in the river Ilm, of one of the ladies at the Weimar court early in 1778. Herder paid Goethe the compliment that if German poetry is to become genuine folk poetry, it must follow Goethe's lead in this ballad.

None of Goethe's ballads is as well known as **9**. It was written for a musical play in 1782 and its theme taken from Herder's translation of a Danish folk song. *Erlkönig* (actually "alder king") is a mistranslation of Danish *ellerkonge*, "elfin king." It is to be noted how closely the meter reflects the mood throughout. A reassuring line like "My son, the mist is on the plain" (eight syllables) is to be compared with such a menacing line as "I love you, your comeliness charms me, my boy!" (eleven syllables). A translator must observe such nuances. The model for this little masterpiece was the Scottish ballad "Edward." Action is everything. The reader is implicated right at the start by the dramatic question; the landscape seems vaguely eerie and shadowy and is tied in skilfully with the ride and with the child's hallucinations.

10 is one of the products of the so-called "ballad year" of 1797, during which Goethe and Schiller, close friends since 1794, vied with one another in composing ballads. The idea of the poem is taken from a tale of the late Greek writer Lucian, as translated by Wieland. Goethe succeeds admirably in suggesting the incessant flow of water and the awkwardness of the animated broomstick. **11**, also in a lighter mood, was written in 1813 and occasioned by a joke once played on a small boy by Goethe's son August.

12 is another product of the "ballad year" of 1797. A "bayadere" is a professional Hindu dancing girl. The ballad is influenced by Kalidasa's *Sakuntala* (500 A.D.) but follows a legend related by a certain Abraham Roger in 1663, as told in Sonnerat's *Journey to India* (*Voyage aux Indes*). Goethe invented only the girl's suicide at the end. His art here is more studied and deliberate than in such ballads as "King in Thule" and "King of the Elves." Even the metrics, with the shift from stately trochees to the more tripping dactyls, illustrate this. Perhaps this ballad, as well as "The Bride of Corinth," written in the same year but not included here, may be used for a comparison with Schiller's ballads, such as "The Diver" (*Der Taucher*) and "The Cranes of Ibycus" (*Die Kraniche des Ibykus*). Goethe prefers folk legend and fairy tale materials, Schiller historical or pseudo-historical subjects that point some ethical lesson or teach divine omnipotence. Goethe stays closer to nature, and at times he demonizes it. Moreover, Schiller's ballads are almost purely dramatic; Goethe's fuse lyric, epic, and dramatic elements.

13 illustrates Goethe's knack for turning an occasional poem into one of deeper, lasting significance. Written for the Berlin singing society of his friend, the composer Zelter, in 1810, as a revision of a poem by Goethe's secretary Riemer, this song was meant to be a belated tribute to the popular Queen Louise of Prussia on her thirty-fourth (and last) birthday in March of that year. But the only reference to her is the "vision, a godly one" at the end, which any singer not a Goethe scholar would interpret in his own way. The effective refrain "ergo bibamus" (Latin for "so let us drink") was a favorite expression with the teacher and schoolman Basedow, in whose company Goethe made an excursion on the Rhine in 1774. The song has crept into some German masonic song books. To achieve the swing, the translator must observe that the refrain regularly has nine syllables, the other lines eleven each.

14, though expressing a sentiment already voiced by Pindar and echoed by Giordano Bruno in the sixteenth century, is one of Goethe's most quoted epigrams. 15 was composed in 1795 and is a thorough revision of a similar poem by a certain Friederike Brun, which Zelter had set to music. Occasionally Goethe took delight in impressing his own stamp upon the work of others (see II, 2 and IX, 5). Margaret's song in *Faust*, "Incline, o Maiden,/ Thou sorrow-laden" (Bayard Taylor's rendering) is based upon a folk song, too, a fact which is apparently unknown to the commentators. 15 is to be sung by a girl. Written, it seems, in 1795, both 16 and 17, which complement each other, are probably reminiscent of Goethe's crossing to Sicily in 1787. Aeolus in 17 is the master of the winds in Greek mythology, who holds them imprisoned with "the troublesome bond."

18-20 are exceptional in having no clearly discernible relationship to Goethe's own experience. Zelter had 18 in his possession early in 1802, but it may be older. It is written in the favorite meter and wistful mood of German folk songs, which also strongly influenced Heine twenty years later. 19, composed in 1796 for a German adaptation of an Italian opera, might be mistaken for a pastoral poem of the rococo period. Originally it had fifteen additional lines, but these now serve as a separate poem, "The Converted Girl" (*Die Bekehrte*). Thyrsis is a conventional name for a shepherd in Greek and Roman pastoral poetry. 20, written probably in 1810, ends on the happy note of the lovers' reunion. "Corn" is here used in the European sense of grain in general.

21, finally, composed about the turn of the century, is one of the finest of the twenty-seven sonnets of Goethe. At first repelled by the sonnet as too artificial a form, he later mastered it. He begins the poem with the idea that nature (spontaneous poetry) and art (the sonnet form) seem to be incongruous. But these become symbols for nature, or freedom, and art, or law, in general, which are found, after all, to be quite compatible and complementary. Thus the poem serves to express a profound conviction of the mature poet. The last two lines are often quoted.

Chapter VII

By the summer of 1786 Goethe had tired of his duties and life at the Weimar court. Instead of returning home from his vacation in Karlsbad (now Karlovy Vary in Czechoslovakia), he headed straight for Italy, informing the duke, but not his other friends, of his plans. He remained away for almost two years, spent most of his time in Rome, but visited also Verona, Venice, Ferrara, Bologna, Naples, and Sicily. The journey did much to mature him for classicism. The "Roman Elegies," in elegiac couplets (hexameter—pentameter), were written between 1787 and 1790 and reflect the poet's experiences and feelings there, and possibly also an Italian liaison. Most of them were probably penned after his return to Weimar in 1788. Another new love which he now found in Weimar is also involved.

When Goethe returned home, he was received warmly enough by his duke, but Charlotte and many others among his neighbors were cool toward him. This coolness became a chill when he, now thirty-nine and inured to the less restrained Italian way of living, took into his home a young girl who had just turned twenty-three. Christiane Vulpius, charming in her way, but with little education, soon entered into a "conscience marriage" with him and bore him five children, of whom only the eldest, August, lived. Thus, without perhaps meaning to be, he was drawn by circumstances into the responsibilities of domestic life. In extenuation it can only be said that he met them fairly well and legalized the alliance in 1806, when Napoleon's troops were plundering Weimar.

The "Venetian Epigrams" (our 5 is the third) were for the most part composed on his second journey to Italy in 1790, where he was to meet and escort the duchess mother Anna Amalia. But this was not as carefree and happy a journey as the first had been. That he longed to be home, appears clearly from our 5. The duchy of Saxe-Weimar was indeed small— smaller than the state of Rhode Island—and Weimar itself had only 6,000 inhabitants at the time. As early as 1776 the duke had presented Goethe with the "Gartenhaus" already referred to in Chapter IV (poem 3). By the time of this Venetian Epigram, *The Sorrows of Young Werther* had already been translated into six languages. Paintings on glass depicting Werther and Lotte (i.e. Charlotte, the heroine), made in China for the European trade, had been brought to Germany as early as 1779.

In Italy Goethe became interested in the life of the notorious mountebank Cagliostro and his part in the scandalous affair of the diamond necklace, in which a cardinal, a countess, and Queen Marie Antoinette herself were involved in 1785. Goethe's comedy *The Grand Cophta* (*Der Grosskophta*) revolves around it. In 6 and 7 he expounds bits of cynical wisdom worthy of Cagliostro and the "Cophta." Merlin was the magician of Arthurian legend.

Chapter VIII

Early in life Goethe was attracted to what we call the Far and Middle East, their literature and civilization. The Bible, especially the Books of Moses and Ruth, and the Song of Songs, the Sakuntala, the Koran, the Arabian Nights, the Book of Kabas, the epic *Medshnun and Leila*, and the work of Saadi became familiar to him. In 1808 Friedrich Schlegel's *On the Language and Wisdom of the Hindus* (*Ueber die Sprache und Weisheit der Indier*) came out, and in 1814 he read the *Divan* (meaning "gathering" or "council room"), a collection of poems by the Persian poet Hafis (fourteenth century), in the translation of Hammer-Purgstall. In Hafis Goethe found a kindred spirit, who had also lived, as he was now living, in a period of turmoil and war.

The presence of French, Austrian, Prussian, and Russian troops in Weimar in 1813 disturbed Goethe greatly, and he escaped from the times by immersing himself first in Chinese, and then in Persian literature. His own *West-Easterly Divan* (1814-1815), published in 1819, represents an attempt at a joyous fusion of Western and Eastern, German and Persian, philosophies. He wrote much of it in the region along or near the Rhine, at Wiesbaden, Frankfort, and Heidelberg. His feminine inspiration, which he always needed, came from Marianne von Willemer (née Jung), the charming young fiancée and soon after wife of a Frankfort banker. The best of the poems, planned to appear in twelve books, but not completed, were inspired by, and veiledly addressed to, her, and indeed about half a dozen have since been proved to be responses from her pen.

In modern literature, Stefan George's poems perhaps come closest to the language of the *West-Easterly Divan*. But the Eastern element is not nearly as authentic as the Western. For Goethe, though, the poems served as a thermal "bath of poetic rejuvenation," as one German critic puts it. Their keynote is activity, their nature proverbial. Rooted in the romantic movement of their time, they have never become widely popular.

1, though not incorporated in the collection, is at the head of the explanatory notes which Goethe prepared. 2 refers directly to the upheavals of the Napoleonic era, from which Goethe makes a *hegira*, or flight, as Mohammed had done from Mecca. Chiser, the warden of the fountain of life, offered Hafis a drink to assure him of eternal fame as a poet. The *houris* were the nymphs of the Mohammedan Paradise. 3 paraphrases the Koran: "The West and the East are Allah's." The thought in 5 is taken from a work of Saadi. 6, written in 1814, before Goethe met Marianne, develops a theme suggested by Hafis, but enriched by the classical theme of psyche, the human soul, seeking immortality as a butterfly, consumed by the torch of Eros, or love. In Goethe's poem the moth and flame, originally symbolizing love's yearning, express a longing for a reunion

with the Divine. The underlying idea of "die, then live all over"
is that of the continual metamorphosis of the individual—his
rebirth—in which physical death is only an incident. This is
to Goethe part of the natural processes of life. Note how the
meter changes in the last stanza. The "you" in stanza 2 is ad-
dressed to the moth, and the "strange feelings" are the moth's
desire for the flame, in which it, after physical birth and pro-
creation, seeks higher union.

10, addressed to Marianne, was written in Heidelberg and
suggested by the maturing chestnuts on the castle grounds.

The poets of Islam attribute ninety-nine other appellations
to Allah, such as All-merciful, All-wise. In 11 Goethe addresses
his Suleika (Marianne) in similar terms, using two "All" com-
pounds in each stanza, except the last. 12 was published a few
years after Goethe's death.

Chapter IX

In our last chapter, IX, Old Age, all the poems, except 20,
date from the last twenty years of the poet's life, during which
his wife and son and most of his friends and associates, includ-
ing the duke (since 1815 grand duke), preceded him in death.
Additional poems of this period, including those in VIII, have
appeared in previous chapters.

Schiller had died on May 9, 1805, at the age of forty-five,
after a long illness. His loss was a severe blow to Goethe, who
was himself just recovering from a serious illness. He did not
attend the obsequies.

On August 10 of that year, at Lauchstädt, the summer theatre
of Duke Karl August, a dramatic presentation of Schiller's
poem "The Song of the Bell" (*Das Lied von der Glocke*) was
given. This was followed by a reading of Goethe's "Epilog,"
(our IX, 1) for which the last two lines of Schiller's poem
served as a prelude. At that time the poem had only ten stan-
zas. Two stanzas, as well as an expansion of one into the
present stanzas 5 and 6, were supplied later, hence the refer-
ence to "ten years" in the last stanza. In its present form the
poem is a product of Goethe's later years. The "young, the
princely pair" refers to the marriage of Karl Friedrich, son of
Karl August, to Maria Paulowna, a daughter of Czar Paul of
Russia, in 1804. For this occasion Schiller wrote his lyric play
The Homage of the Arts (*Die Huldigung der Künste*). Stanza

3, line 1, and stanza 4 refer to his decision in 1804 not to settle in Berlin. The reference to the "storm and tide" (stanza 4) is to his early struggles against poverty and persecution. Stanza 6 refers to Philip II of Spain, depicted in Schiller's drama *Don Carlos* (1787), and to Wallenstein and Gustavus Adolphus in the Thirty Years' War, as portrayed in *Wallenstein* (1799). Stanza 9 refers to Schiller's illness of May, 1791, when he suffered hemorrhages and difficulty in breathing—early signs of the pulmonary disease to which he succumbed fourteen years later.

For twenty-one years Schiller's remains rested in a churchyard vault with the remains of others, but in 1826 they were exhumed. Although even then there was doubt as to the identity of Schiller's skull, Goethe was satisfied that the skull which he apostrophizes in our no. 2, was Schiller's (this has since been further questioned). On September 17, 1826, when the skull was temporarily deposited with ceremony in the grand ducal library, Goethe again was absent, but a week later he had the skull brought to his home, where he wrote this poem. He had not been present in the "charnel house," as he says. The reference to himself as an "adept" (line 15) refers to his studies in phrenology. The "shape" in line 18 is Schiller's skull, while the "ocean" (line 24) is the sea of life, or creative nature, constantly evolving better forms. In the last four lines of the poem Goethe expresses the idea that God, here identified with nature (as in Spinoza), invests material things with qualities of the spirit. The form of the poem is influenced by Dante.

In 3, also written in the 'twenties, we note the esthetic attraction that the interior of a church had for Goethe, who has been called "the great heathen." This "great heathen" was so unpagan that at sixty-five he penned the strongly affirmative lines:

> The man who senses God, I praise.
> He'll never resort to evil ways.*

Obviously he pins his faith on a God of love and suggests that the doctrine of hereditary sin cannot have a place in His scheme of things. About five years later he adds the thought that too often men have blasphemed God by their warped conceptions of Him:

---

* Wer Gott ahnet, ist hoch zu halten,
Denn er wird nie im Schlechten walten.

As is a man, so is his God.
No wonder God sometimes seems odd.**

4, dated 1828, must refer to the French translation of a collection of his poems, *Poésies de Goethe*, published in 1825 by a
Madame Panckouke. Goethe always felt flattered by such a
compliment from abroad (see **VII, 5**).

5 is found in a letter written to Christiane, since 1806 his
wife, on a short journey in 1813, and refers to his "discovery"
of her in 1788, just twenty-five years before. Like **II, 2**, and
VI, 15, it is a reworking of some unrelated verses of a minor
poet. Again Goethe has succeeded in making a little masterpiece of such a product.

Christiane died three years later, on June 6, 1816. Her
passing evoked the following touching lines:

> O sun, you are striving in vain
> To shine through the clouds that are massing!
> My life's entire gain
> Is this: to lament her passing.***

Dated August 25, 1828, 6 was sent to Marianne von Willemer
two months later from Dornburg castle near Jena, to which
Goethe retired after the death of the grand duke in June. In
sending it to her, he reminded her of their agreement, years
ago, to think of each other at the time of full moon. Marianne
replied that she had admired the moon that night and had been
reminded of Goethe's earlier song to the moon (**IV, 8**). 7,
written a month later at Dornburg, deals with three different
times of day, morning, noon, and sundown. In addition to
these two, Goethe wrote several other poems at Dornburg, all
praised by critics for their clear, sublime expression and their
sense of yearning for love and foreboding of death.

But Marianne was not Goethe's last love. He spent the
summer of 1821 in Marienbad (now Marianske Lazne) in Bohemia (now Czechoslovakia), which had only three years before
been established as a spa. There he met a charming young

** Wie einer ist, so ist sein Gott,
   Darum ward Gott so oft zu Spott.
*** Du versuchst, o Sonne, vergebens,
    Durch die düstern Wolken zu scheinen!
    Der ganze Gewinn meines Lebens
    Ist, ihren Verlust zu beweinen.

girl of seventeen, Ulrike von Levetzow, with whom he fell in love. He returned to Marienbad and Ulrike in 1822 and again in 1823, and at the age of seventy-four seriously contemplated marriage, an idea which he sadly renounced after he had been rejected at Karlsbad, where he followed Ulrike and her mother in August of 1823. His poem "Elegie," written after the final farewell, but not included here, laments his plight and sings of his renunciation. However, the following lines were addressed to Ulrike during that last summer.

August, 1823
You've held me captive quite a while,
But now I sense new life in this:
A lovely mouth gives us a friendly smile
When it has granted us a kiss.

September 10, 1823
Close by the thermal spring is where you tarry,
That causes conflict deep inside of me;
For how can you whom in my heart I carry
Be anywhere but where I'd have you be?*

Throughout his long life, especially during his later years, Goethe wrote thousands of epigrams and sayings. Of greatest appeal for us is 12, on America. At the time of the American War of Independence and again in 1818, when an improved map of the American continent appeared, he showed interest in America. This was again revealed when Prince Bernhard, son of Karl August, returned in 1826 from a fifteen months' journey to the New World with a diary, and again in 1827, when he read Alexander von Humboldt's work on Cuba and Colombia. His notion that the New World lacks basalt and volcanic formations is, of course, erroneous.

In the three poems, 18-20, Goethe expresses his mature views

---

* **August 1823**
Du hattest längst mir's angetan,
Doch jetzt gewahr' ich neues Leben:
Ein süsser Mund blickt uns gar freundlich an,
Wenn er uns einen Kuss gegeben.

10. September 1823
Am heissen Quell verbringst du deine Tage,
Das regt mich auf zu innerm Zwist;
Denn wie ich dich so ganz im Herzen trage,
Begreif' ich nicht, wie du wo anders bist.

of life, and man's relationship to nature. He has made vast
strides since the audacious days of "Prometheus Speaks" (III,
2), and yet such a poem as IV, 6, shows that the germs of his
later creed were already present at an early date. In 18 and 19
his pantheism, acquired as early as 1768-1770 on his return
home from Leipzig, finds expression. It was inculcated in him
by his mother's pietist friend, Susanna von Klettenberg, by his
friend Fritz Jacobi, by his reading of Giordano Bruno and,
later, Schelling. Except for Spinoza, few influences upon him
were stronger. He believed firmly that God works not from
without, as a creator of nature (as the Deists believed), but
from within, as the Universal Principle. In lines 9ff. of 18 he
expresses the view that at best human beings can define the
Infinite only through symbols, and cannot understand even
primitive living organisms, except to say that they are tied up
with Infinity. The second section of the poem is a line-for-line
paraphrase of a statement by Bruno. The date of 18 is 1817.

In 19, composed in 1821, Goethe pictures himself as a com-
municant of nature and the universe, which are entities breath-
ing the spirit of God. The world is not static, but is constantly
reshaping itself. Many a man has happily found his place in,
and his proper relation to, infinity and the universe. When he
does, his will is assimilated to that of nature, and all conflict
between man and the outside world vanishes. Permeated with
the spirit of the "world process," we must take part in the un-
ending task of creation. What came to pass at the time of
Creation is constantly in a state of flux by virtue of this "world
process." The last stanza has given rise to different interpre-
tations. It seems to mean: Nothing in creation keeps its origi-
nal form. Everything must perish in its particular, momen-
tary configuration, so that it may attain a new, higher devel-
opment.

Although 20 was written in the early years of the nineteenth
century, it logically belongs with 18 and 19. Again Goethe as-
serts that the world is not everlasting being, but everlasting
becoming, transformation. Men, too, change and then die, but
the creative works of the human genius endure. The "floods"
we see in line 15 refer to the constant flux described by the Greek
philosopher Heraclitus. But since this tide is constantly dif-
ferent, no man will swim in it more than once. Beginning and
ending of things must merge into an endless cycle of life. The

final four lines once more sum up the meaning: In the midst of change and flux everywhere, the creations of the human spirit alone are permanent.

21, written and first printed in 1817, became the motto for the collection "God and World" (*Gott und Welt*) in 1827. It may be considered, in a sense, a restatement of the philosophy embedded in the second part of *Faust*.

22, one of Goethe's last poems, is found in Act V of the second part of *Faust*, not published until after his death in 1832. It is sung by Lynceus, the tower-keeper, one of the Argonauts famed for the sharpness of his vision. But Lynceus is Goethe of the keen brown-black eyes; he too eyed and observed the world in all its phases and confirmed it as only a man can do who identifies himself with nature.

* * * * * *

Whoever has read and digested a representative selection of Goethe's poems will at least have made a good start in becoming familiar with his creed and art, which are essentially one. This creed and art were rooted in the soil of nature, but man and his life on earth—the fulcrum of nature's creative drive—remain the measure of all things. Man's dignity as man cannot and should not be debased, so long as he clings to his faith in the essential goodness of the Unknowable. This is perhaps the supreme lesson of Goethe's life and thought, with their restless originative activity, all-embracing interests, zest for living, and devotion to love as a constant source of inspiration.

CHAPTER I. STUDENT DAYS IN LEIPZIG

1. DIE FREUDEN

Es flattert um die Quelle
Die wechselnde Libelle,
Mich freut sie lange schon;
Bald dunkel und bald helle,
Wie der Chamäleon,
Bald rot, bald blau,
Bald blau, bald grün;
O dass ich in der Nähe
Doch ihre Farben sähe!

Sie schwirrt und schwebet, rastet nie!
Doch still, sie setzt sich an die Weiden.
Da hab' ich sie! Da hab' ich sie!
Und nun betracht' ich sie genau,
Und seh' ein traurig dunkles Blau—

So geht es dir, Zergliederer deiner Freuden!

2. GLÜCK UND TRAUM

Du hast uns oft im Traum gesehen
Zusammen zum Altare gehen,
Und dich als Frau, und mich als Mann.
Oft nahm ich wachend deinem Munde
In einer unbewachten Stunde,
So viel man Küsse nehmen kann.

Das reinste Glück, das wir empfunden,
Die Wollust mancher reichen Stunden
Floh wie die Zeit mit dem Genuss.
Was hilft es mir, dass ich geniesse?
Wie Träume fliehn die wärmsten Küsse,
Und alle Freude wie ein Kuss.

1. THE JOYS

Over the pool a spry
And changing dragon fly
Was long my source of fun;
Now dark, now bright, she charms the eye,
A true chameleon,
Now red, now blue,
Now blue, now green;
O that I, closer by,
Her colors all could spy!

She buzzes, hovers, takes no rest!
There! Now to willows she's directed.
I've caught her, object of my quest!
And then, examining her hue,
I see a dark and sorry blue—

So fares a man when joys he has dissected!

2. HAPPINESS AND DREAM

In dreams you've often seen us stand
Before the altar hand in hand,
And you as bride, as bridegroom me.
And from your lips, how oft in waking,
When no one watched us, I was taking
As many kisses as can be.

The purest joy that life has in it,
The thrill of many a precious minute
Fled like the hours with joy and bliss.
What gain to me are all such blisses?
Like dreams they flee, these warmest kisses,
And every pleasure like a kiss.

CHAPTER II. FRIEDERIKE BRION AND SESENHEIM

1. MAILIED

Wie herrlich leuchtet
Mir die Natur!
Wie glänzt die Sonne!
Wie lacht die Flur!

Es dringen Blüten
Aus jedem Zweig
Und tausend Stimmen
Aus dem Gesträuch.

Und Freud' und Wonne
Aus jeder Brust.
O Erd', o Sonne!
O Glück, o Lust!

O Lieb', o Liebe!
So golden schön,
Wie Morgenwolken
Auf jenen Höhn!

Du segnest herrlich
Das frische Feld,
Im Blütendampfe
Die volle Welt.

O Mädchen, Mädchen,
Wie lieb' ich dich!
Wie blinkt dein Auge!
Wie liebst du mich!

So liebt die Lerche
Gesang und Luft,
Und Morgenblumen
Den Himmelsduft,

Wie ich dich liebe
Mit warmem Blut,
Die du mir Jugend
Und Freud' und Mut

Zu neuen Liedern
Und Tänzen gibst.
Sei ewig glücklich,
Wie du mich liebst!

1. SONG OF MAY

How brilliantly Nature
Beams upon me!
The glowing sunlight!
The laughing lea!

From every branch
The blossoms burst,
A thousand voices
From every hurst.

And joy and rapture
From every breast.
O Earth, o Sunshine,
O joy, o zest!

O love, o loving,
So golden bright,
Like clouds of morning
On yonder height!

You bless with glory
The fields of green,
With blossoms' fragrance
The earth's rich sheen.

What love, o maiden,
I have for you!
Your eye is beaming
With love-light too.

So loves the skylark
Her song on high,
So morning blossoms
The balmy sky,

As I love you
With warmth athrill,
Who youth and spirit
And joy instil

For ever new songs
And dances free.
Be always happy
As you love me!

2. HEIDENRÖSLEIN

Sah ein Knab' ein Röslein stehn,
Röslein auf der Heiden,
War so jung und morgenschön,
Lief er schnell, es nah zu sehn,
Sah's mit vielen Freuden.
Röslein, Röslein, Röslein rot,
Röslein auf der Heiden.

Knabe sprach: Ich breche dich,
Röslein auf der Heiden!
Röslein sprach: Ich steche dich,
Dass du ewig denkst an mich,
Und ich will's nicht leiden.
Röslein, Röslein, Röslein rot,
Röslein auf der Heiden.

Und der wilde Knabe brach
's Röslein auf der Heiden;
Röslein wehrte sich und stach,
Half ihm doch kein Weh und Ach,
Musst' es eben leiden.
Röslein, Röslein, Röslein rot,
Röslein auf der Heiden.

3. MIT EINEM GEMALTEN BAND

Kleine Blumen, kleine Blätter
Streuen mir mit leichter Hand
Gute junge Frühlingsgötter
Tändelnd auf ein luftig Band.

Zephyr, nimm's auf deine Flügel,
Schling's um meiner Liebsten Kleid!
Und so tritt sie vor den Spiegel
All in ihrer Munterkeit.

Sieht mit Rosen sich umgeben,
Selbst wie eine Rose jung:
Einen Blick, geliebtes Leben!
Und ich bin belohnt genung.

2. ROSE IN THE HEATHER

Boy once saw a rosebud rare,
Rosebud in the heather,
Fresh as morning's glow and fair,
Near he ran to see her there,
Saw the rose with pleasure.
Rosebud, little rosebud red,
Rosebud in the heather.

"I will pick you, rose," said he,
"Rosebud in the heather!"
"I will prick you, boy," said she,
"That you'll always think of me.
I'll not grant your pleasure."
Rosebud, little rosebud red,
Rosebud in the heather.

And the rash boy broke the rose,
Rosebud in the heather.
With her thorns she dared oppose.
Useless all her ah's and oh's,
Had to grant his pleasure.
Rosebud, little rosebud red,
Rosebud in the heather.

3. WITH A PAINTED RIBBON

Little leaves I see and flowers
Strewn for me with sportive hand
By young gods with springtime powers
Lightly on a wafted band.

Zephyr, on your soft wings bear it,
Wind it round my sweetheart's dress,
And before the glass she'll wear it,
Marked by all her sprightliness.

Sees herself in rose-filled bower,
She too like a rosebud sweet.
Grant me, dear, one glance this hour!
My reward will be complete.

Fühle, was dies Herz empfindet,
Reiche frei mir deine Hand,
Und das Band, das uns verbindet,
Sei kein schwaches Rosenband!

4. BLINDE KUH

O liebliche Therese!
Wie wandelt gleich ins Böse
Dein offnes Auge sich!
Die Augen zugebunden,
Hast du mich schnell gefunden,
Und warum fingst du eben mich?

Du fasstest mich aufs beste
Und hieltest mich so feste,
Ich sank in deinen Schoss.
Kaum warst du aufgebunden,
War alle Lust verschwunden,
Du liessest kalt den Blinden los.

Er tappte hin und wieder,
Verrenkte fast die Glieder,
Und alle foppten ihn.
Und willst du mich nicht lieben,
So geh' ich stets im Trüben,
Wie mit verbundnen Augen, hin.

5. WILLKOMMEN UND ABSCHIED

Es schlug mein Herz: geschwind zu Pferde!
Es war getan fast eh' gedacht.
Der Abend wiegte schon die Erde,
Und an den Bergen hing die Nacht;
Schon stand im Nebelkleid die Eiche,
Ein aufgetürmter Riese, da,
Wo Finsternis aus dem Gesträuche
Mit hundert schwarzen Augen sah.

Feel what my heart too is feeling,
Freely let me clasp your hand;
Let the ribbon round us reeling
Be no slender painted band!

4. BLIND MAN'S BUFF

Theresa, though you charm me,
How soon your eyes alarm me
When they're no longer bound!
With eyes blindfolded tightly
You captured me so sprightly,
And why was I the one you found?

Adroitly then you grasped me
And held me fast and clasped me,
I sank upon your knee.
But once they had untied you,
No more was joy beside you,
You coldly set the blind man free.

In vain he groped and pointed,
His limbs almost disjointed;
They laughed his plight to scorn.
If love you're still not showing,
In darkness I'll be going,
As if with blinded eyes forlorn.

5. GREETING AND FAREWELL

To horse! my pounding heart kept crying,
No sooner was it thought than done.
In evening's lap the earth was lying,
And on the peaks the night was spun;
Already clad in mist, the giant,
The oak, stood towering eerily,
Where darkness from the copse defiant
Turned many somber eyes on me.

Der Mond von einem Wolkenhügel
Sah kläglich aus dem Duft hervor,
Die Winde schwangen leise Flügel,
Umsausten schauerlich mein Ohr;
Die Nacht schuf tausend Ungeheuer,
Doch frisch und fröhlich war mein Mut:
In meinen Adern welches Feuer!
In meinem Herzen welche Glut!

Dich sah ich, und die milde Freude
Floss von dem süssen Blick auf mich:
Ganz war mein Herz an deiner Seite
Und jeder Atemzug für dich.
Ein rosenfarbes Frühlingswetter
Umgab das liebliche Gesicht,
Und Zärtlichkeit für mich—ihr Götter!
Ich hofft' es, ich verdient' es nicht!

Doch ach, schon mit der Morgensonne
Verengt der Abschied mir das Herz:
In deinen Küssen welche Wonne!
In deinem Auge welcher Schmerz!
Ich ging, du standst und sahst zur Erden
Und sahst mir nach mit nassem Blick:
Und doch, welch Glück, geliebt zu werden!
Und lieben, Götter, welch ein Glück!

The moon, from clouded hill appeared
And frowned upon the hazy lea,
The wind by quiet wings was steered
And whirred with horror over me;
To countless shapes the night was turned,
My feelings though were fresh and gay,
For in my veins, what ardor burned,
And in my heart, what glowing lay!

I saw you, felt the joyful sweetness
Of your kind eyes come over me.
My heart was yours in all completeness,
And every breath was yours to be.
'A day in spring with roses blended,
It wreathed your face in loveliness,—
Tenderness, gods, for me intended,
Deserving no such hoped-for bliss!

But soon at sunlight's earliest minute
My heart grows faint to say goodbye.
Your kisses' warmth, what rapture in it,
What sorrow lingers in your eye!
I went; your head was lowered in sadness,
You watched me go, in deep distress.
And yet, to be so loved, what gladness!
To love, o gods, what happiness!

CHAPTER III. EARLY DAYS OF STORM AND STRESS

1. AN SCHWAGER KRONOS

Spude dich, Kronos!
Fort den rasselnden Trott!
Bergab gleitet der Weg;
Ekles Schwindeln zögert
Mir vor die Stirne dein Haudern.
Frisch, holpert es gleich,
Über Stock und Steine den Trott
Rasch ins Leben hinein!

Nun schon wieder
Den eratmenden Schritt
Mühsam Berg hinauf!
Auf denn, nicht träge denn,
Strebend und hoffend hinan!

Weit, hoch, herrlich der Blick
Rings ins Leben hinein!
Vom Gebirg zum Gebirg
Schwebet der ewige Geist,
Ewigen Lebens ahndevoll.

Seitwärts des Überdachs Schatten
Zieht dich an,
Und ein Frischung verheissender Blick
Auf der Schwelle des Mädchens da.—
Labe dich—Mir auch, Mädchen,
Diesen schäumenden Trank,
Diesen frischen Gesundheitsblick!

Ab denn, rascher hinab!
Sieh, die Sonne sinkt!
Eh' sie sinkt, eh' mich Greisen
Ergreift im Moore Nebelduft,
Entzahnte Kiefer schnattern
Und das schlotternde Gebein—

Trunknen vom letzten Strahl
Reiss mich, ein Feuermeer
Mir im schäumenden Aug',
Mich geblendeten, taumelnden
In der Hölle nächtliches Tor!

1. TO COACHMAN CRONOS

Hasten now, Cronos!
Away with clattering trot!
Downhill beckons the road;
Nauseous dizziness steals
Over my brow at your driving.
Quick, though the ride's rough,
Over stick and stones on a trot,
Forward swift into life!

And now again
The breath-taking pace
Up the toilful grade!
Up, up, not sluggish now,
Striving, hoping, ascend!

Wide, high, glorious view
Round about upon life!
From summit to summit
The spirit eternal pervades,
Boding a life without end.

Sidewards a portico shaded
Lures your eye,
And a glance that offers refreshment
On a maiden's threshold there.—
Go, be refreshed!—Give me too,
Maiden, this foaming draft,
Give me this glance of cheer and health!

Downgrade, quicker descend!
See, the sun will set!
Ere it sets, ere the fog-drifts
Snatch me, grown old, in the moorland,
Chattering with jaws that are toothless,
Rattling my tottering frame—

Drunk with the sun's last ray,
Swirl me with seas of fire
Glowing still in my eye,
Swirl me blinded and staggering
Down to the nightlike portal of hell!

Töne, Schwager, ins Horn,
Rassle den schallenden Trab,
Dass der Orkus vernehme: wir kommen!
Dass gleich an der Türe
Der Wirt uns freundlich empfange.

2. PROMETHEUS

Bedecke deinen Himmel, Zeus,
Mit Wolkendunst
Und übe, dem Knaben gleich,
Der Disteln köpft,
An Eichen dich und Bergeshöhn—
Musst mir meine Erde
Doch lassen stehn
Und meine Hütte, die du nicht gebaut,
Und meinen Herd,
Um dessen Glut
Du mich beneidest.

Ich kenne nichts Ärmeres
Unter der Sonn' als euch, Götter!
Ihr nähret kümmerlich
Von Opfersteuern
Und Gebetshauch
Eure Majestät
Und darbtet, wären
Nicht Kinder und Bettler
Hoffnungsvolle Toren.

Da ich ein Kind war,
Nicht wusste, wo aus noch ein,
Kehrt' ich mein verirrtes Auge
Zur Sonne, als wenn drüber wär'
Ein Ohr, zu hören meine Klage,
Ein Herz, wie meins,
Sich des Bedrängten zu erbarmen.

Wer half mir
Wider der Titanen Übermut?
Wer rettete vom Tode mich,

Blow, coachman, blow your horn,
Clatter with echoing trot,
That all Orcus may hear: We're coming!
That there in the doorway
Our host may graciously greet us.

2. PROMETHEUS SPEAKS

O cover up your heaven, Zeus,
With hazy mist,
And practice, like a lad
Beheading thistles,
On oak trees and on mountain heights—
My earth you must perforce
Leave standing yet,
And this my hut that you did not erect,
And my own hearth,
Whose radiant fire
Excites your envy.

What is more pitiable
Under the sun than you, o gods!
You nourish meagerly
Your power majestic
On votive tribute
And prayerful breath,
And you'd starve unless
Both children and beggars
Were not such hope-filled fools.

When I was a child
And knew not whither to go,
I turned my deluded vision
Sunward, as if beyond
There were an ear to hear complaining,
A heart like mine,
Feeling some pity for the oppressed.

Who helped me
Against the Titans' towering pride?
Who rescued me from death,

Von Sklaverei?
Hast du nicht alles selbst vollendet,
Heilig glühend Herz?
Und glühtest jung und gut,
Betrogen, Rettungsdank
Dem Schlafenden da droben?

Ich dich ehren? Wofür?
Hast du die Schmerzen gelindert
Je des Beladenen?
Hast du die Tränen gestillet
Je des Geängsteten?
Hat nicht mich zum Manne geschmiedet
Die allmächtige Zeit
Und das ewige Schicksal,
Meine Herrn und deine?

Wähntest du etwa,
Ich sollte das Leben hassen,
In Wüsten fliehen,
Weil nicht alle
Blütenträume reiften?

Hier sitz' ich, forme Menschen
Nach meinem Bilde,
Ein Geschlecht, das mir gleich sei:
Zu leiden, zu weinen,
Zu geniessen und zu freuen sich—
Und dein nicht zu achten,
Wie ich!

3. GANYMED

Wie im Morgenglanze
Du rings mich anglühst,
Frühling, Geliebter!
Mit tausendfacher Liebeswonne
Sich an mein Herz drängt
Deiner ewigen Wärme
Heilig Gefühl,
Unendliche Schöne!

From slavery?
Have you not done it all alone,
Sacred glowing heart?
Young and good you glowed,
But duped, with thanks for help
To him who slept in heaven?

I honor *you*? For what?
Have you ever soothed the sorrows
Of one by burdens crushed?
Have you ever dried the teardrops
Of him with terror struck?
Have I not been forged into manhood
By all-powerful Time,
And by Fate everlasting,
Who are my lords and yours?

Could you perchance think
That I should hate this life
And flee to deserts,
Since not every
Budding vision ripened?

I sit here, forming mortals
After my image,
A race to resemble me:
To weep and to suffer,
To enjoy life and to feel delight—
And never to heed you,
Even as I!

3. GANYMED

How in the morning's splendor
You beam upon me,
Springtime beloved!
With thousandfold delights of love,
O infinite beauty,
Into my heart wells
The holy feeling
Of your eternal warmth!

Dass ich dich fassen möcht'
In diesen Arm!

Ach an deinem Busen
Lieg' ich, schmachte,
Und deine Blumen, dein Gras
Drängen sich an mein Herz.
Du kühlst den brennenden
Durst meines Busens,
Lieblicher Morgenwind,
Ruft drein die Nachtigall
Liebend nach mir aus dem Nebeltal.

Ich komm'! ich komme!
Wohin? Ach, wohin?

Hinauf! Hinauf strebt's.
Es schweben die Wolken
Abwärts, die Wolken
Neigen sich der sehnenden Liebe.
Mir! Mir!
In eurem Schosse
Aufwärts!
Umfangend umfangen!
Aufwärts an deinen Busen,
Alliebender Vater!

4. AN BELINDEN

Warum ziehst du mich unwiderstehlich,
Ach, in jene Pracht?
War ich guter Junge nicht so selig
In der öden Nacht?

Heimlich in mein Zimmerchen verschlossen,
Lag im Mondenschein,
Ganz von seinem Schauerlicht umflossen,
Und ich dämmert' ein.

Träumte da von vollen goldnen Stunden
Ungemischter Lust,
Hatte schon dein liebes Bild empfunden
Tief in meiner Brust.

That I might hold you close
Within these arms!

Ah, upon your bosom
I lie, languished,
And your flowers, your grass
Press in close to my heart.
You slake the blazing hot
Thirst of my bosom,
Exquisite morning wind,
When soft the nightingale
Yearningly calls me from misty vales.

I come, I'm coming,
But whither, ah whither?

Up, upward my urge!
The cloudbanks are floating
Earthwards, the cloudbanks
Bow before the yearning of lovers.
To me, to me!
In your lap floating
Upwards!
Embraced and embracing,
Upward into Thy bosom,
All-loving Father!

4. TO BELINDA

Why entice me with resistless power
To that flood of light?
Was I not, good lad, in bliss each hour
Of the lonely night?

Locked into my chamber secretly,
In the moon's pale ray,
With its eerie light surrounding me,
Lulled in sleep I lay.

There I dreamed of golden hours that showed
Rapture at its best,
Even then your charming image glowed
Deep within my breast.

Bin ich's noch, den du bei so viel Lichtern
An dem Spieltisch hältst?
Oft so unerträglichen Gesichtern
Gegenüber stellst?

Reizender ist mir des Frühlings Blüte
Nun nicht auf der Flur:
Wo du, Engel, bist, ist Lieb' und Güte,
Wo du bist, Natur.

5. NEUE LIEBE, NEUES LEBEN

Herz, mein Herz, was soll das geben?
Was bedränget dich so sehr?
Welch ein fremdes, neues Leben!
Ich erkenne dich nicht mehr.
Weg ist alles, was du liebtest,
Weg, warum du dich betrübtest,
Weg dein Fleiss und deine Ruh—
Ach, wie kamst du nur dazu!

Fesselt dich die Jugendblüte,
Diese liebliche Gestalt,
Dieser Blick voll Treu und Güte,
Mit unendlicher Gewalt?
Will ich rasch mich ihr entziehen,
Mich ermannen, ihr entfliehen,
Führet mich im Augenblick,
Ach, mein Weg zu ihr zurück.

Und an diesem Zauberfädchen,
Das sich nicht zerreissen lässt,
Hält das liebe, lose Mädchen
Mich so wider Willen fest:
Muss in ihrem Zauberkreise
Leben nun auf ihre Weise.
Die Verändrung, ach, wie gross!
Liebe! Liebe! lass mich los!

Is it I you've held to gaming places
With the lights ablaze,
There to see unbearable grimaces
All around me gaze?

Budding fields in springtime's lovely splendor
Give no fairer view.
Angel, where you are, love's care is tender,
There is nature too!

5. NEW LOVE, NEW LIFE

Heart, my heart, o why this feeling?
This oppression deep and sore?
Odd new life you are revealing,
Strange, I know your ways no more.
Gone is all that made you gladder,
Gone the grief that made you sadder,
Gone your zeal and peaceful bliss.
Ah, how could you come to this?

Does her form so charmed and youthful,
Like a newly opening flower,
Do her eyes so kindly truthful
Fetter you with endless power?
If at once no more I'd see her,
If I brace myself and flee her,
In a trice my feet will strain
To return to her again.

By this thread with magic laden
Which I cannot tear at all,
That beloved wanton maiden
Holds me, a reluctant thrall.
In her magic circle standing,
I must live at her commanding.
Ah, how great the change in me!
Love, o love, o set me free!

6. AUF DEM SEE

Und frische Nahrung, neues Blut
Saug' ich aus freier Welt:
Wie ist Natur so hold und gut,
Die mich am Busen hält!
Die Welle wieget unsern Kahn
Im Rudertakt hinauf,
Und Berge, wolkig himmelan,
Begegnen unserm Lauf.

Aug', mein Aug', was sinkst du nieder?
Goldne Träume, kommt ihr wieder?
Weg, du Traum! so gold du bist:
Hier auch Lieb' und Leben ist.

Auf der Welle blinken
Tausend schwebende Sterne,
Weiche Nebel trinken
Rings die türmende Ferne;
Morgenwind umflügelt
Die beschattete Bucht,
Und im See bespiegelt
Sich die reifende Frucht.

7. VOM BERGE

Wenn ich, liebe Lili, dich nicht liebte,
Welche Wonne gäb' mir dieser Blick!
Und doch, wenn ich, Lili, dich nicht liebte,
Fänd' ich hier und fänd' ich dort mein Glück?

8. HERBSTGEFÜHL

Fetter grüne, du Laub,
Am Rebengeländer
Hier mein Fenster herauf!
Gedrängter quellet,
Zwillingsbeeren, und reifet
Schneller und glänzend voller!

6. ON THE LAKE

And rich refreshment, strength renewed,
I draw from freedom's breast:
How kind is nature, and how good,
That holds me as her guest!
The billows rock our skiff and try
To match the pulsing oars,
And hilltops, cloudlike toward the sky,
Advance to meet our course.

Eye, mine eye, why droop forlorn?
Golden dreams, are you reborn?
Go, dream, golden though you be:
Here, too, love and life I see.

On the waves are twinkling
Stars in a flickering shower,
Softly mists are drinking
Heights that around us tower;
Morning winds are directed
Toward the shaded cove,
In the lake are reflected
Ripening fruits of the grove.

7. FROM THE HILLTOP

If I loved you not, beloved Lili,
What delight would this wide vista bring!
And yet if I loved you not, my Lili,
Where would I find joy in anything?

8. MOOD OF AUTUMN

Thrive more lushly, you leaves,
On arbor of grapevines
Over my window-sill!
Swell more, more densely,
Twin-born clusters, and ripen
Swifter, and gleam more richly!

Euch brütet der Mutter Sonne
Scheideblick; euch umsäuselt
Des holden Himmels
Fruchtende Fülle;
Euch kühlet des Mondes
Freundlicher Zauberhauch,
Und euch betauen, ach!
Aus diesen Augen
Der ewig belebenden Liebe
Vollschwellende Tränen.

9. AN LILI

Dezember 1775

Holde Lili, warst so lang
All mein' Lust und all mein Sang,
Bist nun all mein Schmerz und doch
All mein Sang bist du noch.

10. AN LILI

Weimar, 1776

Im holden Tal, auf schneebedeckten Höhen
War stets dein Bild mir nah:
Ich sah's um mich in lichten Wolken wehen,
Im Herzen war mir's da.
Empfinde hier, wie mit allmächt'gem Triebe
Ein Herz das andre zieht—
Und dass vergebens Liebe
Vor Liebe flieht.

You're brooded by nurturing sunshine's
Farewell glance; round you rustles
The gracious heavens'
Fruit-bearing fulness;
You're cooled by the moonlight's
Friendly magical breath,
And you're moistened, alas,
From these very eyelids
Of love's ever life-giving dew
By rich welling teardrops.

9. TO LILI

December, 1775

Lovely Lili, you were long
All my joy and all my song.
Now you're all my grief, and still,
Lili, all my songs you fill.

10. TO LILI

Weimar, 1776

In pleasant dale, on heights by snowbanks bounded
I saw your image fair.
In light, transparent clouds I often found it,
And in my heart 'twas there.
In this, see with what full endeavor
Heart draws heart mightily—
And that true love can never
From true love flee.

11. JÄGERS ABENDLIED

Im Felde schleich' ich still und wild,
Gespannt mein Feuerrohr,
Da schwebt so licht dein liebes Bild,
Dein süsses Bild mir vor.

Du wandelst jetzt wohl still und mild
Durch Feld und liebes Tal,
Und ach, mein schnell verrauschend Bild,
Stellt sich dir's nicht einmal?

Des Menschen, der die Welt durchstreift
Voll Unmut und Verdruss,
Nach Osten und nach Westen schweift,
Weil er dich lassen muss.

Mir ist es, denk' ich nur an dich,
Als in den Mond zu sehn;
Ein stiller Friede kommt auf mich,
Weiss nicht, wie mir geschehn.

12. REZENSENT

Da hatt' ich einen Kerl zu Gast,
Er war mir eben nicht zur Last;
Ich hatt' just mein gewöhnlich Essen,
Hat sich der Kerl pumpsatt gefressen,
Zum Nachtisch, was ich gespeichert hatt'.
Und kaum ist mir der Kerl so satt,
Tut ihn der Teufel zum Nachbar führen
Über mein Essen zu räsonnieren:
„Die Supp' hätt' können gewürzter sein,
Der Braten brauner, firner der Wein."
Der Tausendsakerment!
Schlagt ihn tot den Hund! Er ist ein Rezensent.

11. HUNTER'S EVENING SONG

Through fields I'm roving hushed and wild,
My gun is cocked and free,
Where clear I see your face, dear child,
Your lovely face I see.

Perhaps you're strolling hushed and mild
Through field and dale we've known.
Are you not by my face beguiled,
Though dim it soon has grown?

The face of one who wanders on
Chagrined and mortified.
To East and then to West he's gone
Since he must leave your side.

In thinking but of you, I feel
As when the moon I see;
Over me peace appears to steal,
What's happening to me?

12. THE REVIEWER

A fellow was my guest one day,
Not too much of a pest I'd say;
I merely served my usual food,
The fellow devoured as much as he could.
Dessert? Whatever was on my shelf.
When, hardly had he gorged himself,
The devil led him to my neighbor,
My food to criticize and belabor:
"The soup could have had more spice and savor,
The roast lacked browning, the young wine flavor."
A thousand curses and boos!
Strike him dead, the dog, because he writes reviews!

CHAPTER IV. WEIMAR

1. RASTLOSE LIEBE

Dem Schnee, dem Regen,
Dem Wind entgegen,
Im Dampf der Klüfte,
Durch Nebeldüfte,
Immer zu! Immer zu!
Ohne Rast und Ruh!

Lieber durch Leiden
Möcht' ich mich schlagen,
Als so viel Freuden
Des Lebens ertragen.
Alle das Neigen
Von Herzen zu Herzen,
Ach, wie so eigen
Schaffet das Schmerzen!

Wie, soll ich fliehen?
Wälderwärts ziehen?
Alles vergebens!
Krone des Lebens,
Glück ohne Ruh,
Liebe, bist du!

2. AN CHARLOTTE VON STEIN

Weimar, 14. April 1776

Warum gabst du uns die tiefen Blicke,
Unsre Zukunft ahnungsvoll zu schaun,
Unsrer Liebe, unserm Erdenglücke
Wähnend selig nimmer hinzutraun?
Warum gabst uns, Schicksal, die Gefühle,
Uns einander in das Herz zu sehn,
Um durch all' die seltenen Gewühle
Unser wahr Verhältnis auszuspähn?

Ach, so viele tausend Menschen kennen,
Dumpf sich treibend, kaum ihr eigen Herz;
Schweben zwecklos hin und her und rennen
Hoffnungslos in unversehnen Schmerz;
Jauchzen wieder, wenn der schnellen Freuden

1. RESTLESS LOVE

Rain, wind and snow
I brave as I go,
In misty clifts,
Through fog that drifts,
On, on, and away!
Without stop or stay!

Better to struggle
Through sorrow and pain
Than to endure
Life's happiest gain.
All this affection
That heart feels for heart
Takes the direction
Of buffet and smart!

What, shall I flee,
In forests to be?
Vain were the quest!
Joy without rest—
Life's crown ever new—
Love, is but you!

2. TO CHARLOTTE VON STEIN

Weimar, April 14, 1776

Why with insight deep did you endow us
Presciently to see our future days,
In despair that love will not allow us
Happiness that gives us hopeful rays?
Fate, why did you bless us with the feelings
That should probe each other's heart and mood,
That despite life's rare, tumultuous dealings
We could find how our relations stood?

Ah, so many thousands, dully drifting
On through life, their own hearts barely know;
To and fro they move, and idly shifting
In their hopeless, unexpected woe,
Then exult again when sunrise hovers

Unerwart'te Morgenröte tagt.
Nur uns armen liebevollen beiden
Ist das wechselseit'ge Glück versagt,
Uns zu lieben, ohn' uns zu verstehen,
In dem andern sehn, was er nie war,
Immer frisch auf Traumglück auszugehen
Und zu schwanken auch in Traumgefahr.

Glücklich, den ein leerer Traum beschäftigt!
Glücklich, dem die Ahnung eitel wär'!
Jede Gegenwart und jeder Blick bekräftigt
Traum und Ahnung leider uns noch mehr.
Sag', was will das Schicksal uns bereiten?
Sag', wie band es uns so rein genau?
Ach du warst in abgelebten Zeiten
Meine Schwester oder meine Frau.

Kanntest jeden Zug in meinem Wesen,
Spähtest, wie die reinste Nerve klingt,
Konntest mich mit e i n e m Blicke lesen,
Den so schwer ein sterblich Aug' durchdringt.
Tropftest Mässigung dem heissen Blute,
Richtetest den wilden irren Lauf,
Und in deinen Engelsarmen ruhte
Die zerstörte Brust sich wieder auf;
Hieltest zauberleicht ihn angebunden
Und vergaukeltest ihm manchen Tag.
Welche Seligkeit glich jenen Wonnestunden,
Da er dankbar dir zu Füssen lag,
Fühlt' sein Herz an deinem Herzen schwellen,
Fühlte sich in deinem Auge gut,
Alle seine Sinnen sich erhellen
Und beruhigen sein brausend Blut!

Und von allem dem schwebt ein Erinnern
Nur noch um das ungewisse Herz,
Fühlt die alte Wahrheit ewig gleich im Innern,
Und der neue Zustand wird ihm Schmerz.
Und wir scheinen uns nur halb beseelet,
Dämmernd ist um uns der hellste Tag.
Glücklich, dass das Schicksal, das uns quälet,
Uns doch nicht verändern mag!

With swift joys in rosy-colored light.
Only we, unfortunate two lovers,
Cannot claim that mutual delight:
Our love is not bare of understanding,
Nor that sees the friend as he can't be,
In a dream-bliss always newly landing,
Even dreaming dreams so dangerously.

Happy he in empty dreamland moving!
Happy whose forebodings seem untrue!
Every moment, every glance is proving
Dream and boding doubly for us two.
Tell me, what has fate in preparation?
Say, how could it bind us so in life?
Ah, you were in some past generation
Either sister or my wedded wife.

Every trait in me you knew, and feature,
Saw how every nerve and thought react,
With a glance you could make out my nature—
Powers that mortal eyes have often lacked.
Gave my heated blood more moderation,
Guided well my mad, wild course at length,
And my breast, distraut with desperation,
In your angel arms renewed its strength;
With your magic touch you held him captured,
Conjuring the hours and days away.
Ah, what bliss could match those happy hours enraptured,
When in thanks before your feet he lay,
Felt his heart upon your bosom glowing,
Felt his worth reflected in your gleam,
All his senses more perceptive growing,
While his blood now flowed in calmer stream.

And of this now only recollection
Hovers still around the groping heart,
Keeping yet the truth of old in like affection,
While the present state brings grief and smart.
So we seem not more than partly living,
Dimly round us lurks the brightest day.
Happy we, that fate, such torture giving,
Cannot change us as it may.

3. HOFFNUNG

Schaff', das Tagwerk meiner Hände,
Hohes Glück, dass ich's vollende!
Lass, o lass mich nicht ermatten!
Nein, es sind nicht leere Träume:
Jetzt nur Stangen, diese Bäume
Geben einst noch Frucht und Schatten.

4. GESANG DER GEISTER ÜBER DEN WASSERN

Des Menschen Seele
Gleicht dem Wasser:
Vom Himmel kommt es,
Zum Himmel steigt es,
Und wieder nieder
Zur Erde muss es,
Ewig wechselnd.

Strömt von der hohen,
Steilen Felswand
Der reine Strahl,
Dann stäubt er lieblich
In Wolkenwellen
Zum glatten Fels,
Und leicht empfangen
Wallt er verschleiernd,
Leisrauschend
Zur Tiefe nieder.

Ragen Klippen
Dem Sturz entgegen,
Schäumt er unmutig
Stufenweise
Zum Abgrund.

Im flachen Bette
Schleicht er das Wiesental hin,
Und in dem glatten See
Weiden ihr Antlitz
Alle Gestirne.

3. HOPE

Fortune, let the work be ended,
Once for my two hands intended!
Let my vigor show no want!
No, 'tis not an empty dream:
Though these trees like poles now seem,
Fruit and shade some day they'll grant.

4. SONG OF THE SPIRITS OVER THE WATERS

The soul of man
Is like the water:
It comes from heaven,
To heaven it rises,
And strains again
To earth perforce,
Ever changing.

When from the lofty,
Rocky steepness
The pure foam streams,
It sprays in lovely
And cloudlike billows
On shiny rock,
And caught up lightly
It rolls on, veil-like,
Soft-plashing
To lower places.

Where crags project,
Its fall resisting,
It foams in anger,
Steps descending
Down the abyss.

In shallow stream-bed
Through grassy meadows it creeps,
And in the quiet lake
All constellations
Pasture their image.

Wind ist der Welle
Lieblicher Buhler;
Wind mischt vom Grund aus
Schäumende Wogen.

Seele des Menschen,
Wie gleichst du dem Wasser!
Schicksal des Menschen,
Wie gleichst du dem Wind!

5. GRENZEN DER MENSCHHEIT

Wenn der uralte,
Heilige Vater
Mit gelassener Hand
Aus rollenden Wolken
Segnende Blitze
Über die Erde sät,
Küss' ich den letzten
Saum seines Kleides,
Kindliche Schauer
Treu in der Brust.

Denn mit Göttern
Soll sich nicht messen
Irgend ein Mensch.
Hebt er sich aufwärts
Und berührt
Mit dem Scheitel die Sterne,
Nirgends haften dann
Die unsichern Sohlen,
Und mit ihm spielen
Wolken und Winde.

Steht er mit festen,
Markigen Knochen
Auf der wohlgegründeten
Dauernden Erde,
Reicht er nicht auf,
Nur mit der Eiche
Oder der Rebe
Sich zu vergleichen.

Wind is the wavelet's
Amorous lover;
Wind stirs from bed-rock
Foam-whitened billows.

Soul of mankind,
How like to the water!
Fate of mankind,
How like to the wind!

5. LIMITATIONS OF MAN

When the primeval
Heavenly Father
With a tranquil hand
From hurrying clouds
Sows flashes of blessing
Over the earth below,
I kiss the extremest
Hem of His garment,
Filial shudders
True in my breast.

For with the gods
No man should ever
Seek to compare.
If he rises upward
There to touch
The stars with his forehead,
Nowhere can rest
His uncertain feet,
And storm-clouds and tempest
Will make sport of him.

If he stand firm
With sturdy robustness
On the well supported
Permanent earth-sphere,
He will fall short
So much as to vie
In vain with the oak
Or with the vine.

Was unterscheidet
Götter von Menschen?
Dass viele Wellen
Vor jenen wandeln,
Ein ewiger Strom:
Uns hebt die Welle,
Verschlingt die Welle,
Und wir versinken.

Ein kleiner Ring
Begrenzt unser Leben,
Und viele Geschlechter
Reihen sie dauernd
An ihres Daseins
Unendliche Kette.

6.   DAS GÖTTLICHE

Edel sei der Mensch,
Hilfreich und gut!
Denn das allein
Unterscheidet ihn
Von allen Wesen,
Die wir kennen.

Heil den unbekannten
Höhern Wesen,
Die wir ahnen!
Sein Beispiel lehr' uns
Jene glauben.

Denn unfühlend
Ist die Natur:
Es leuchtet die Sonne
Über Bös' und Gute,
Und dem Verbrecher
Glänzen wie dem Besten
Der Mond und die Sterne.

Wind und Ströme,
Donner und Hagel
Rauschen ihren Weg

What can distinguish
Gods from the mortals?
That many waves
Before them travel,
An infinite stream:
We're raised by the wave,
Devoured by the wave,
And we sink downward.

A tiny ring
Sets bounds to our life,
And gods link forever
Long generations
To the unending chain
Of their deathless existence.

6. THE GODLIKE

Noble let man be,
Helpful and good!
For that alone
Distinguishes him
From all the creatures
Of our knowledge.

Hail to all the unknown
Loftier beings
Whom we divine!
May man's example
Teach faith in them.

For unfeeling
Is Nature itself.
The radiant sunlight
Shines on good and evil,
The moon and stars
Beam on the villain,
Beam on the best of us.

Wind and torrent,
Thunder and hailstorm
Roar upon their way,

Und ergreifen
Vorüber eilend
Einen um den andern.

Auch so das Glück
Tappt unter die Menge,
Fasst bald des Knaben
Lockige Unschuld,
Bald auch den kahlen
Schuldigen Scheitel.

Nach ewigen, ehrnen,
Grossen Gesetzen
Müssen wir alle
Unseres Daseins
Kreise vollenden.

Nur allein der Mensch
Vermag das Unmögliche:
Er unterscheidet,
Wählet und richtet;
Er kann dem Augenblick
Dauer verleihen.

Er allein darf
Den Guten lohnen,
Den Bösen strafen,
Heilen und retten,
Alles Irrende, Schweifende
Nützlich verbinden.

Und wir verehren
Die Unsterblichen,
Als wären sie Menschen,
Täten im grossen,
Was der Beste im kleinen
Tut oder möchte.

Der edle Mensch
Sei hilfreich und gut!
Unermüdet schaff' er
Das Nützliche, Rechte,
Sei uns ein Vorbild
Jener geahneten Wesen!

And they take hold
Of one or the other
As onward they rush.

Likewise Fortune
Gropes among the masses,
Grips now the young lad's
Innocent forelock,
Now the bald crown
Guilty of sinning.

Obeying great changeless
Iron-bound statutes,
We must all of us
Round out the cycle
Of our existence.

Only man alone
Can do the impossible.
He can decide,
He chooses and judges,
Can give to the moment
Lasting endurance.

He alone can
Reward the good man,
Punish the wicked,
Heal men and rescue,
Usefully joining
What's erring and straying.

And we revere
The powers immortal
As if they were human,
Performing in greatness
What the best of us
Punily try or achieve.

Let noble man
Be helpful and good!
Tirelessly doing
The useful and righteous—
A prefiguration
Of beings we only divine.

7. ZUEIGNUNG

Der Morgen kam; es scheuchten seine Tritte
Den leisen Schlaf, der mich gelind umfing,
Dass ich, erwacht, aus meiner stillen Hütte
Den Berg hinauf mit frischer Seele ging;
Ich freute mich bei einem jeden Schritte
Der neuen Blume, die voll Tropfen hing:
Der junge Tag erhob sich mit Entzücken,
Und alles war erquickt, mich zu erquicken.

Und wie ich stieg, zog von dem Fluss der Wiesen
Ein Nebel sich in Streifen sacht hervor,
Er wich und wechselte, mich zu umfliessen,
Und wuchs geflügelt mir ums Haupt empor.
Des schönen Blicks sollt' ich nicht mehr geniessen,
Die Gegend deckte mir ein trüber Flor:
Bald sah ich mich von Wolken wie umgossen
Und mit mir selbst in Dämmrung eingeschlossen.

Auf einmal schien die Sonne durchzudringen,
Im Nebel liess sich eine Klarheit sehn.
Hier sank er, leise sich hinabzuschwingen,
Hier teilt' er steigend sich um Wald und Höhn.
Wie hofft' ich ihr den ersten Gruss zu bringen!
Sie hofft' ich nach der Trübe doppelt schön.
Der luft'ge Kampf war lange nicht vollendet,
Ein Glanz umgab mich, und ich stand geblendet.

Bald machte mich, die Augen aufzuschlagen,
Ein innrer Trieb des Herzens wieder kühn,
Ich konnt' es nur mit schnellen Blicken wagen,
Denn alles schien zu brennen und zu glühn.
Da schwebte, mit den Wolken hergetragen,
Ein göttlich Weib vor meinen Augen hin:
Kein schöner Bild sah ich in meinem Leben,
Sie sah mich an und blieb verweilend schweben.

Kennst du mich nicht? sprach sie mit einem Munde,
Dem aller Lieb' und Treue Ton entfloss:
Erkennst du mich, die ich in manche Wunde
Des Lebens dir den reinsten Balsam goss?
Du kennst mich wohl, an die, zu ew'gem Bunde,

7. DEDICATION

The morning came, dispelling on its way
The gentle sleep that lightly held me still;
I woke with vigor for the new-born day
And left my quiet cot to climb the hill;
With fresh new flowers and dew that on them lay,
At every step high joys my spirit fill.
Young day arose, new ecstacies it bore me,
And all things were restored, there to restore me.

And as I climbed, the meadow mist, now churning,
In stripes rose gently from the river's bed;
With yielding, shifting motion upward turning,
Its wings soon grew and floated round my head.
I looked in vain, no lovely view discerning,
For over it a dull grey veil was spread.
Soon everywhere I looked the scene was clouded
And by myself in twilight I was shrouded.

Then suddenly the sun found penetration,
And through the mist there grew a shining light.
The fog arose, in gentle dissipation,
It curled and parted here round woods and height.
O how I hoped with early salutation
To greet the sun, returning doubly bright!
This spectacle for long I watched and minded.
A gleam broke round me, and I stood there blinded.

But soon, to lift my eyes, an urgent feeling
That gripped my heart had once more made me bold;
I looked, but only rapid glances stealing,
For everything now burned and blazed like gold.
Then clouds came floating past my head, revealing
A woman, like a goddess to behold.
My eyes by fairer sight were ne'er elated.
She looked at me and tarried there and waited.

"You know me not?" her gentle words resounded,
Whose unfeigned love my confidence restored;
"O recognize me who, when you were wounded,
Oft on your sores the purest balm have poured?
You know me well, with me a bond you founded

Dein strebend Herz sich fest und fester schloss.
Sah ich dich nicht mit heissen Herzenstränen
Als Knabe schon nach mir dich eifrig sehnen?

Ja! rief ich aus, indem ich selig nieder
Zur Erde sank, lang hab' ich dich gefühlt:
Du gabst mir Ruh, wenn durch die jungen Glieder
Die Leidenschaft sich rastlos durchgewühlt;
Du hast mir wie mit himmlischem Gefieder
Am heissen Tag die Stirne sanft gekühlt;
Du schenktest mir der Erde beste Gaben,
Und jedes Glück will ich durch dich nur haben!

Dich nenn' ich nicht. Zwar hör' ich dich von vielen
Gar oft genannt, und jeder heisst dich sein,
Ein jedes Auge glaubt auf dich zu zielen,
Fast jedem Auge wird dein Strahl zur Pein.
Ach, da ich irrte, hatt' ich viel Gespielen,
Da ich dich kenne, bin ich fast allein:
Ich muss mein Glück nur mit mir selbst geniessen,
Dein holdes Licht verdecken und verschliessen.

Sie lächelte, sie sprach: Du siehst, wie klug,
Wie nötig war's, euch wenig zu enthüllen!
Kaum bist du sicher vor dem gröbsten Trug,
Kaum bist du Herr vom ersten Kinderwillen,
So glaubst du dich schon Übermensch genug,
Versäumst die Pflicht des Mannes zu erfüllen!
Wie viel bist du von andern unterschieden?
Erkenne dich, leb' mit der Welt in Frieden!

Verzeih mir, rief ich aus, ich meint' es gut!
Soll ich umsonst die Augen offen haben?
Ein froher Wille lebt in meinem Blut,
Ich kenne ganz den Wert von deinen Gaben.
Für andre wächst in mir das edle Gut,
Ich kann und will das Pfund nicht mehr vergraben!
Warum sucht' ich den Weg so sehnsuchtsvoll,
Wenn ich ihn nicht den Brüdern zeigen soll?

Und wie ich sprach, sah mich das hohe Wesen
Mit einem Blick mitleid'ger Nachsicht an;
Ich konnte mich in ihrem Auge lesen,

To keep your heart in ever close accord.
Did I not watch your boyish tear-drops fall
And know it was for me that you would call?"

"Ah yes," I cried, with sudden rapture kneeling
Upon the ground, "long since I've felt you near;
Whene'er I sensed the restless passion stealing
Through my young limbs, 'twas you that gave me cheer;
Your heavenly wings—how soft and cool the feeling!—
Refreshed my brow when summer's fields were sear;
You blessed me with the fairest gifts of living,
And every boon I crave but through your giving.

"I name you not. I hear you by too many
Too often named, each calling you his own;
All eyes to you aspire, yet hardly any
Can stand your splendor, when by you outshone.
Ah, while I strayed I had companions many,
But since I know you, I'm almost alone:
My joy is only mine, I cannot share it,
I dare not show your gracious light and bare it."

She smiled, she spoke: "You realize how wise,
How needful 'twas that much I'm still withholding!
Deceit you've scarcely learned to recognize,
For childish whims you still deserve a scolding.
You think you're superman enough, despise
The duties of a man and their upholding!
How much are you distinguished from the others?
Go, know yourself, and call all men your brothers!"

"Forgive me," I exclaimed, "my plan was good!
Shall I with open eyes be yet unseeing?
A happy purpose animates my blood,
I know your gifts, the value of their being.
For other men I cherish noble Good,
From earth my buried talent I'll be freeing!
Why have I sought the path, why longed to know it,
If to my brothers I am not to show it?"

And as I spoke, that lofty being viewed me
Indulgently—a sympathetic sight;
Her shining eye with higher power endued me

Was ich verfehlt und was ich recht getan.
Sie lächelte, da war ich schon genesen,
Zu neuen Freuden stieg mein Geist heran:
Ich konnte nun mit innigem Vertrauen
Mich zu ihr nahn und ihre Nähe schauen.

Da reckte sie die Hand aus in die Streifen
Der leichten Wolken und des Dufts umher;
Wie sie ihn fasste, liess er sich ergreifen,
Er liess sich ziehn, es war kein Nebel mehr.
Mein Auge konnt' im Tale wieder schweifen,
Gen Himmel blickt' ich, er war hell und hehr.
Nur sah ich sie den reinsten Schleier halten,
Er floss um sie und schwoll in tausend Falten.

Ich kenne dich, ich kenne deine Schwächen,
Ich weiss, was Gutes in dir lebt und glimmt!
—So sagte sie, ich hör' sie ewig sprechen,—
Empfange hier, was ich dir lang' bestimmt!
Dem Glücklichen kann es an nichts gebrechen,
Der dies Geschenk mit stiller Seele nimmt:
Aus Morgenduft gewebt und Sonnenklarheit,
Der Dichtung Schleier aus der Hand der Wahrheit.

Und wenn es dir und deinen Freunden schwüle
Am Mittag wird, so wirf ihn in die Luft!
Sogleich umsäuselt Abendwindes Kühle,
Umhaucht euch Blumen-Würzgeruch und Duft.
Es schweigt das Wehen banger Erdgefühle,
Zum Wolkenbette wandelt sich die Gruft,
Besänftiget wird jede Lebenswelle,
Der Tag wird lieblich, und die Nacht wird helle.

So kommt denn, Freunde, wenn auf euren Wegen
Des Lebens Bürde schwer und schwerer drückt,
Wenn eure Bahn ein frischerneuter Segen
Mit Blumen ziert, mit goldnen Früchten schmückt,
Wir gehn vereint dem nächsten Tag entgegen!
So leben wir, so wandeln wir beglückt.
Und dann auch soll, wenn Enkel um uns trauern,
Zu ihrer Lust noch unsre Liebe dauern.

To see where I had erred and done the right.
She smiled, and with her healing power imbued me.
My spirit found the heights of new delight.
With heartfelt confidence I now grew bolder
To near her presence, closer to behold her.

Her hand into the mist she then extended,
Which from the haze and fleecy clouds would pour;
By her the mist was lightly apprehended
And drawn at pleasure; 'twas a cloud no more.
Again into the vale my eye descended,
Then upward to the radiant sky did soar;
The purest gauze of white I saw her holding,
Her form in countless flowing lines enfolding.

"I know you, know each weakness of your spirit,
I know the Good that in you has not slept."
Thus spoke her voice, forever shall I hear it.
"Come, take here what for you I long have kept!
A favored one need feel no lack, nor fear it,
If he this gift with silent heart accept:
Woven of sun, of mist at dawn that lingers,
The veil of Poetry from Truth's own fingers.

"And when your friends and you should feel oppressed
With heat at noon, then toss it in the air!
The evening breeze will soon be at your breast,
To waft around you flowery fragrance fair.
The surge of earthly fears will be suppressed,
From vault to bed of clouds you will repair;
Life's billows will be quieted before you,
Day grow more lovely, night hang brighter o'er you."

Come, then, you friends, when, on your journey faring,
Life's burden grows more onerous day by day,
Or fresh and new-found blessings you are bearing,
With flowers and golden fruits to cheer your way,
Let all of us the morrow's road be sharing,
To live and walk contented while we may!
And then, when mourned by later-born with sadness,
Our love shall still endure to give them gladness.

8. AN DEN MOND

Füllest wieder Busch und Tal
Still mit Nebelglanz,
Lösest endlich auch einmal
Meine Seele ganz;

Breitest über mein Gefild
Lindernd deinen Blick,
Wie des Freundes Auge mild
Über mein Geschick.

Jeden Nachklang fühlt mein Herz
Froh- und trüber Zeit,
Wandle zwischen Freud' und Schmerz
In der Einsamkeit.

Fliesse, fliesse, lieber Fluss!
Nimmer werd' ich froh:
So verrauschte Scherz und Kuss,
Und die Treue so.

Ich besass es doch einmal,
Was so köstlich ist!
Dass man doch zu seiner Qual
Nimmer es vergisst!

Rausche, Fluss, das Tal entlang,
Ohne Rast und Ruh,
Rausche, flüstre meinem Sang
Melodien zu!

Wenn du in der Winternacht
Wütend überschwillst,
Oder um die Frühlingspracht
Junger Knospen quillst.

Selig, wer sich vor der Welt
Ohne Hass verschliesst,
Einen Freund am Busen hält
Und mit dem geniesst,

Was, von Menschen nicht gewusst,
Oder nicht bedacht,
Durch das Labyrinth der Brust
Wandelt in der Nacht.

8. TO THE MOON

Filling bush and dale, you cast
Peaceful haze again,
Leaving all my soul at last
Free of toil and strain.

Over my domain you send
Rays that comfort me,
Like the eye with which a friend
Guards my destiny.

Bygone days of bliss and woe
Echo in my soul,
Joy and grief in turn I know,
As alone I stroll.

Stream beloved, flow on, flow on!
Joy I'll never see.
Thus have sport and kisses gone,
Gone is constancy.

Long ago I did possess
Gifts so precious yet!
Man must ever feel distress
That he can't forget.

Stream, through valleys rush along,
Never finding ease.
Rush and whisper to my song
Answering melodies,

When you rage in winter's night
Till you overflow,
Or in springtime sparkle bright
Where young blossoms blow.

He who from the world retires
Free of hate, is blessed,
When a friend's love he inspires,
Sharing at his breast

What, unknown to human ways,
Or not planned aright,
Roams through hearts as in a maze
All the silent night.

9. GUTER RAT

Geschieht wohl, dass man einen Tag
Weder sich noch andre leiden mag,
Will nichts dir nach dem Herzen ein;
Sollt's in der Kunst wohl anders sein?
Drum hetze dich nicht zur schlimmen Zeit,
Denn Füll' und Kraft sind nimmer weit:
Hast in der bösen Stund' geruht,
Ist dir die gute doppelt gut.

10. WONNE DER WEHMUT

Trocknet nicht, trocknet nicht,
Tränen der ewigen Liebe!
Ach, nur dem halbgetrockneten Auge
Wie öde, wie öde die Welt ihm erscheint!
Trocknet nicht, trocknet nicht,
Tränen unglücklicher Liebe!

11. WANDERERS NACHTLIED

Der du von dem Himmel bist,
Alles Leid und Schmerzen stillest,
Den, der doppelt elend ist,
Doppelt mit Erquickung füllest,
Ach, ich bin des Treibens müde!
Was soll all der Schmerz und Lust?
Süsser Friede,
Komm, ach komm in meine Brust!

12. EIN GLEICHES

Über allen Gipfeln
Ist Ruh,
In allen Wipfeln
Spürest du
Kaum einen Hauch;
Die Vögelein schweigen im Walde.
Warte nur, balde
Ruhest du auch.

9. GOOD ADVICE

On certain days, it may be true,
You'll hate all men, including you.
Nothing will seem to please your heart.
Why should it not be so in art?
So don't strain hard on your wretched day;
Full strength is never far away.
If you have rested in evil hours,
The good ones will have twofold powers.

10. SWEETNESS OF SORROW

Never dry, never dry,
Tears of a love that is endless!
Ah, when the eye is but halfway tearless,
How dreary, how dreary the world in its sight!
Never dry, never dry,
Tears of a love that is hopeless.

11. WANDERER'S NIGHT SONG I

Thou that from the heavens art,
Every pain and sorrow stillest,
And the doubly wretched heart
Doubly with refreshment fillest,
Ah, I'm weary with contending!
Why this grief and joyful zest?
Peace, descending,
Come, sweet Peace, into my breast!

12. II

Over every hill
Is repose.
In the trees, you feel,
Scarcely goes
The stir of a breeze.
Hushed birds in the forest are nesting.
Wait, you'll be resting
Soon too like these.

13. ERSTER VERLUST

Ach, wer bringt die schönen Tage,
Jene Tage der ersten Liebe,
Ach, wer bringt nur eine Stunde
Jener holden Zeit zurück!

Einsam nähr' ich meine Wunde,
Und mit stets erneuter Klage
Traur' ich ums verlorne Glück.

Ach, wer bringt die schönen Tage,
Jene holde Zeit zurück!

13.   FIRST LOSS

Who'll bring back fair days that fleeted,
Those sweet days of a young love budding,
Who'll bring back one hour only
Of that time of blissfulness!

Deep the wound I nourish, lonely,
And with outcry oft repeated
I bemoan lost happiness.

Who'll bring back fair days that fleeted,
That sweet time of blissfulness!

CHAPTER V. FROM "WILHELM MEISTER"

1. MIGNON I

Kennst du das Land, wo die Zitronen blühn,
Im dunkeln Laub die Gold-Orangen glühn,
Ein sanfter Wind vom blauen Himmel weht,
Die Myrte still und hoch der Lorbeer steht—
Kennst du es wohl?
                    Dahin! Dahin
Möcht' ich mit dir, o mein Geliebter, ziehn!

Kennst du das Haus? Auf Säulen ruht sein Dach,
Es glänzt der Saal, es schimmert das Gemach,
Und Marmorbilder stehn und sehn mich an:
Was hat man dir, du armes Kind, getan?—
Kennst du es wohl?
                    Dahin! Dahin
Möcht' ich mit dir, o mein Beschützer, ziehn!

Kennst du den Berg und seinen Wolkensteg?
Das Maultier sucht im Nebel seinen Weg,
In Höhlen wohnt der Drachen alte Brut,
Es stürzt der Fels und über ihn die Flut—
Kennst du ihn wohl?
                    Dahin! Dahin
Geht unser Weg; o Vater, lass uns ziehn!

2. MIGNON II

Nur wer die Sehnsucht kennt,
Weiss, was ich leide!
Allein und abgetrennt
Von aller Freude,
Seh' ich ans Firmament
Nach jener Seite.
Ach, der mich liebt und kennt,
Ist in der Weite.
Es schwindelt mir, es brennt
Mein Eingeweide.
Nur wer die Sehnsucht kennt,
Weiss, was ich leide!

1. MIGNON I

You know the country where the lemon grows,
In deep green leaves the golden orange glows?
Soft winds are blowing from the azure sky,
The myrtle stands serene, the laurel high—
You know it well?
                    O there, o there
Would I with you, o my beloved, fare!

You know the house? On columns rest the beams,
The great hall shines, and every chamber gleams,
And marble statues stand and catch my eye:
Poor child, what have men done to you? they sigh—
You know it well?
                    O there, o there
With you, protector, I would gladly fare!

You know the crag, its footpath cloudy grey?
Through fog and mist the mule seeks out its way.
The caverns house the dragons' ancient brood,
The cliffs collapse, and over them the flood—
You know it well?
                    O there, o there
Our pathway goes; o father let us fare!

2. MIGNON II

Only the yearning heart
Knows of my sadness!
Alone and far apart
From joy and gladness
I scan the skies in quest
Of him who left me.
My love, who knows me best,
He has bereft me.
My senses reel, I smart,
Burning with madness.
Only the yearning heart
Knows of my sadness!

3. HARFENSPIELER I

Wer sich der Einsamkeit ergibt,
Ach! der ist bald allein;
Ein jeder lebt, ein jeder liebt
Und lässt ihn seiner Pein.
Ja! lasst mich meiner Qual!
Und kann ich nur einmal
Recht einsam sein,
Dann bin ich nicht allein.

Es schleicht ein Liebender lauschend sacht,
Ob seine Freundin allein?
So überschleicht bei Tag und Nacht
Mich Einsamen die Pein,
Mich Einsamen die Qual.
Ach, werd' ich erst einmal
Einsam im Grabe sein,
Da lässt sie mich allein!

4. HARFENSPIELER II

Wer nie sein Brot mit Tränen ass,
Wer nie die kummervollen Nächte
Auf seinem Bette weinend sass,
Der kennt euch nicht, ihr himmlischen Mächte.

Ihr führt ins Leben uns hinein,
Ihr lasst den Armen schuldig werden,
Dann überlasst ihr ihn der Pein;
Denn alle Schuld rächt sich auf Erden.

3. THE HARPER I

The man who yields to solitude,
Is all too soon alone.
Men live and love as is their mood
And leave him there to groan.
Yes, let me keep my woe!
When once I can but go
In solitude, unknown,
I shall not be alone.

A lover will steal to listen and see
Is the girl he loves alone?
Thus day and night woe silently
Insnares me, lonesome one,
To torture lonesome me.
Ah, when at last I'll be
Beneath the burial stone,
Will grief leave me alone.

4. THE HARPER II

Who never ate his bread with tears,
Who never wept through nightly hours
Upon his bed in grief and fears,
He knows you not, you heavenly Powers.

You lead us into life's estate,
Confuse the wretch in guilt and strife,
Then leave him to his painful fate;
All guilt must be atoned in life.

CHAPTER VI. SONGS, BALLADS, AND A SONNET

1. VORKLAGE

Wie nimmt ein leidenschaftlich Stammeln
Geschrieben sich so seltsam aus!
Nun soll ich gar von Haus zu Haus
Die losen Blätter alle sammeln.

Was eine lange weite Strecke
Im Leben von einander stand,
Das kommt nun unter e i n e r Decke
Dem guten Leser in die Hand.

Doch schäme dich nicht der Gebrechen,
Vollende schnell das kleine Buch:
Die Welt ist voller Widerspruch,
Und sollte sich's nicht widersprechen?

2. AN DIE GÜNSTIGEN

Dichter lieben nicht zu schweigen,
Wollen sich der Menge zeigen.
Lob und Tadel muss ja sein!
Niemand beichtet gern in Prosa,
Doch vertraun wir oft sub Rosa
In der Musen stillem Hain.

Was ich irrte, was ich strebte,
Was ich litt und was ich lebte,
Sind hier Blumen nur im Strauss.
Und das Alter wie die Jugend,
Und der Fehler wie die Tugend
Nimmt sich gut in Liedern aus.

3. DAS VEILCHEN

Ein Veilchen auf der Wiese stand,
Gebückt in sich und unbekannt;
Es war ein herzigs Veilchen.
Da kam eine junge Schäferin
Mit leichtem Schritt und munterm Sinn
Daher, daher,
Die Wiese her, und sang.

1. PRELIMINARY COMPLAINT

A stammering that's warm with passion,
When written down to read, seems strange!
From place to place I'll have to range,
Loose leaves into a sheaf to fashion.

Events in life far separated,
When intervals between them stand,
Will, brought together, close related,
Be laid into the reader's hand.

Heed not the flaws, the book's afflictions,
Complete it now without ado;
The world is inconsistent too.
Should not the book have contradictions?

2. TO THE GENTLE READER

Poets, never silent creatures,
Like to show the crowd their features.
Praise and censure must exist!
Men would not confess in prose,
Secrets, though, they oft disclose
Where serene the Muses tryst.

All my erring, all my striving,
Suffering and life's contriving
Are but flowers in this bouquet.
And old age, like youth's temptations,
Virtues, even aberrations,
All look good when lyres play.

3. THE VIOLET

A violet in the meadow grew,
With drooping head, whom no one knew;
It was a charming flower.
A shepherd maid was making her way
With sprightly step and spirits gay
Along, along,
Across the field with song.

Ach! denkt das Veilchen, wär' ich nur
Die schönste Blume der Natur,
Ach, nur ein kleines Weilchen,
Bis mich das Liebchen abgepflückt
Und an dem Busen matt gedrückt!
Ach nur, ach nur
Ein Viertelstündchen lang!

Ach! aber ach! das Mädchen kam
Und nicht in acht das Veilchen nahm,
Ertrat das arme Veilchen.
Es sank und starb und freut' sich noch:
Und sterb' ich denn, so sterb' ich doch
Durch sie, durch sie,
Zu ihren Füssen doch.

4. FREUDVOLL UND LEIDVOLL

Freudvoll
Und leidvoll,
Gedankenvoll sein,
Langen
Und bangen
In schwebender Pein,
Himmelhoch jauchzend,
Zum Tode betrübt—
Glücklich allein
Ist die Seele, die liebt.

5. DER KÖNIG IN THULE

Es war ein König in Thule
Gar treu bis an das Grab,
Dem sterbend seine Buhle
Einen goldnen Becher gab.

Es ging ihm nichts darüber,
Er leert' ihn jeden Schmaus;
Die Augen gingen ihm über,
So oft er trank daraus.

Ah, mused the violet, could I be
'The fairest flower to grace the lea
For, ah, the shortest hour,
Till by this lovely maid I'm found
And to her bosom crushed and bound!
Could, could I be
For one brief quarter hour!

But oh, but oh, the maiden trod
The violet into the sod,
Saw not the humble flower.
It sank and died in joy complete:
And if I die, my death I meet
Through her, through her,
Beneath her very feet.

4. CHEERFUL AND TEARFUL

Cheerful
And tearful,
In thoughtfulness tense,
Hoping
And groping
In painful suspense,
Exulting to heaven,
In mortal distress—
The lover alone
Knows true happiness.

5. THE KING IN THULE

There was a king in Thule,
Was faithful to the grave,
Whom she that loved him truly
In dying a goblet gave.

Nothing so pleased this lover,
Each feast he drained the cup;
The tears in his eyes ran over
Whenever he held it up.

Und als er kam zu sterben,
Zählt' er seine Städt' im Reich,
Gönnt' alles seinem Erben,
Den Becher nicht zugleich.

Er sass beim Königsmahle,
Die Ritter um ihn her,
Auf hohem Vätersaale
Dort auf dem Schloss am Meer.

Dort stand der alte Zecher,
Trank letzte Lebensglut,
Und warf den heil'gen Becher
Hinunter in die Flut.

Er sah ihn stürzen, trinken
Und sinken tief ins Meer.
Die Augen täten ihm sinken:
Trank nie einen Tropfen mehr.

6. MEINE RUH IST HIN

Meine Ruh ist hin,
Mein Herz ist schwer,
Ich finde sie nimmer
Und nimmermehr.

Wo ich ihn nicht hab',
Ist mir das Grab,
Die ganze Welt
Ist mir vergällt.

Mein armer Kopf
Ist mir verrückt,
Mein armer Sinn
Ist mir zerstückt.

Meine Ruh ist hin,
Mein Herz ist schwer,
Ich finde sie nimmer
Und nimmermehr.

Nach ihm nur schau' ich
Zum Fenster hinaus,

And when he came to dying,
The towns in his realm he enrolled,
His heir no prize denying,
Except that cup of gold.

And at a royal wassail
With all his knights sat he
In the hall of his father's castle
That faces toward the sea.

The old carouser slowly
Stood up, drank life's last glow,
And flung the cup so holy
Into the flood below.

He saw it plunging, drinking
As deep in the sea it sank.
His eyes the while were sinking,
Not a drop again he drank.

6. MY PEACE IS GONE

My peace is gone,
My heart is sore,
I'll find it never
And nevermore.

Where I have him not
The grave's my lot,
My world and all
Has turned to gall.

My poor, poor head
I feel is crazed,
My poor, poor mind
Is torn and dazed.

My peace is gone,
My heart is sore,
I'll find it never
And nevermore.

To see him I watch
At the window seat,

Nach ihm nur geh' ich
Aus dem Haus.

Sein hoher Gang,
Sein' edle Gestalt,
Seines Mundes Lächeln,
Seiner Augen Gewalt,

Und seiner Rede
Zauberfluss,
Sein Händedruck,
Und ach, sein Kuss!

Meine Ruh ist hin,
Mein Herz ist schwer,
Ich finde sie nimmer
Und nimmermehr.

Mein Busen drängt
Sich nach ihm hin,
Ach dürft' ich fassen
Und halten ihn,

Und küssen ihn,
So wie ich wollt',
An seinen Küssen
Vergehen sollt'!

7. DER SÄNGER

Was hör' ich draussen vor dem Tor,
Was auf der Brücke schallen?
Lass den Gesang vor unserm Ohr
Im Saale widerhallen!
Der König sprach's, der Page lief;
Der Knabe kam, der König rief:
Lasst mir herein den Alten!

Gegrüsset seid mir, edle Herrn,
Gegrüsst ihr, schöne Damen!
Welch reicher Himmel! Stern bei Stern!
Wer kennet ihre Namen?

To find him I go
Into the street.

His walk erect,
His stature grand,
The smile of his mouth,
His eyes that command!

His every word's
Enchanting bliss,
The clasp of his hand,
And ah, his kiss!

My peace is gone,
My heart is sore,
I'll find it never
And nevermore.

My bosom craves
To feel him near;
Ah, might I grasp him
And hold him here,

And kiss him oft,
As I desire,
Then on his kisses
I would expire!

7. THE MINSTREL

"Beyond the gate what's that I hear,
Across the drawbridge ringing?
Now let the strains approach our ear
And through the hall be singing!"
So spoke the king, the page-boy sped,
The boy returned, the monarch said:
"Come, let the old man enter!"

"My greeting to each noble knight,
Ladies, to you my greeting!
Star next to star! What heavenly sight.
Their names defy repeating.

Im Saal voll Pracht und Herrlichkeit
Schliesst, Augen, euch: hier ist nicht Zeit,
Sich staunend zu ergötzen.

Der Sänger drückt' die Augen ein
Und schlug in vollen Tönen;
Die Ritter schauten mutig drein,
Und in den Schoss die Schönen.
Der König, dem das Lied gefiel,
Liess, ihn zu ehren für sein Spiel,
Eine goldne Kette holen.

Die goldne Kette gib mir nicht,
Die Kette gib den Rittern,
Vor deren kühnem Angesicht
Der Feinde Lanzen splittern;
Gib sie dem Kanzler, den du hast,
Und lass ihn noch die goldne Last
Zu andern Lasten tragen.

Ich singe, wie der Vogel singt,
Der in den Zweigen wohnet;
Das Lied, das aus der Kehle dringt,
Ist Lohn, der reichlich lohnet.
Doch darf ich bitten, bitt' ich eins:
Lass mir den besten Becher Weins
In purem Golde reichen.

Er setzt' ihn an, er trank ihn aus:
O Trank voll süsser Labe!
O wohl dem hochbeglückten Haus,
Wo das ist kleine Gabe!
Ergeht's euch wohl, so denkt an mich,
Und danket Gott so warm, als ich
Für diesen Trunk euch danke.

8. DER FISCHER

Das Wasser rauscht', das Wasser schwoll,
Ein Fischer sass daran,
Sah nach dem Angel ruhevoll,
Kühl bis ans Herz hinan.

In this resplendent hall sublime
Be closed, my eyes! 'Tis not the time
For me to feast my wonder."

The aged minstrel closed his eyes,
Rich strains of music raising;
The knights looked on in dauntless wise,
Ladies to earth were gazing.
The monarch, happy with the strain,
Bade them bring forth a golden chain,
To be the singer's guerdon.

"The golden chain give not to me,
The chain give to the yeomen,
Splintered in whose bold face will be
The lances of the foemen;
Or give it to your chancellor there,
With other burdens he may bear
This one more golden burden.

"I sing as birds are wont to sing
That live in woodland bowers;
The song that from the throat will ring
Has self-rewarding powers.
One boon I crave, if not too bold:
A draft in cup of purest gold
As my reward be given."

The cup he raised, the cup he quaffed:
"O drink of quickening savor!
O house thrice-blessed, where such a draft
Is deemed a trifling favor!
When fortune smiles, remember me,
And thank the Lord as heartily
As for this cup I thank you."

8. THE FISHERMAN

The water rushed, the water rose,
A fisherman by the sea
Observed his line in deep repose,
Cool to his heart was he.

Und wie er sitzt und wie er lauscht,
Teilt sich die Flut empor:
Aus dem bewegten Wasser rauscht
Ein feuchtes Weib hervor.

Sie sang zu ihm, sie sprach zu ihm:
Was lockst du meine Brut
Mit Menschenwitz und Menschenlist
Hinauf in Todesglut?
Ach wüsstest du, wie's Fischlein ist
So wohlig auf dem Grund,
Du stiegst herunter, wie du bist,
Und würdest erst gesund.

Labt sich die liebe Sonne nicht,
Der Mond sich nicht im Meer?
Kehrt wellenatmend ihr Gesicht
Nicht doppelt schöner her?
Lockt dich der tiefe Himmel nicht,
Das feuchtverklärte Blau?
Lockt dich dein eigen Angesicht
Nicht her in ew'gen Tau?

Das Wasser rauscht', das Wasser schwoll,
Netzt' ihm den nackten Fuss;
Sein Herz wuchs ihm so sehnsuchtsvoll,
Wie bei der Liebsten Gruss.
Sie sprach zu ihm, sie sang zu ihm,
Da war's um ihn geschehn:
Halb zog sie ihn, halb sank er hin
Und ward nicht mehr gesehn.

9. ERLKÖNIG

Wer reitet so spät durch Nacht und Wind?
Es ist der Vater mit seinem Kind;
Er hat den Knaben wohl in dem Arm,
Er fasst ihn sicher, er hält ihn warm.

Mein Sohn, was birgst du so bang dein Gesicht?—
Siehst, Vater, du den Erlkönig nicht?
Den Erlenkönig mit Kron' und Schweif?—
Mein Sohn, es ist ein Nebelstreif.

And as he sits and listens well,
The billow breaks and parts,
And from the waters' churning swell
A dripping woman darts.

She sang to him, she spoke to him:
"Why lure my kind away
With human wit and cunningly
To the deadly blaze of day?
If you could know how blithe and free
The fishes thrive below,
You would descend, with us to be,
And prosperous to grow.

"Do not the sun and moon take on
Refreshment in the sea?
Do not their faces billow-drawn
Loom twice as splendidly?
This sky-like depth, it calls you not,
This dank transfigured blue?
Your mirrored form enthralls you not
To seek the endless dew?

The water rushed, the water rose
And wet his naked feet;
His heart with yearning swells and grows,
As when two lovers meet.
She spoke to him, she sang to him,
And then his fate was plain:
Half drawn by her he glided in
And was not seen again.

9. KING OF THE ELVES

Who's riding so late where winds blow wild?
It is the father grasping his child;
He holds the boy embraced in his arm,
He clasps him snugly, he keeps him warm.

"My son, why cover your face in such fear?"
"You see the elf-king, father? He's near!
The king of the elves with crown and train!"
"My son, the mist is on the plain."

„Du liebes Kind, komm, geh mit mir!
Gar schöne Spiele spiel' ich mit dir;
Manch bunte Blumen sind an dem Strand,
Meine Mutter hat manch gülden Gewand."

Mein Vater, mein Vater, und hörest du nicht,
Was Erlenkönig mir leise verspricht?—
Sei ruhig, bleibe ruhig, mein Kind:
In dürren Blättern säuselt der Wind.

„Willst, feiner Knabe, du mit mir gehn?
Meine Töchter sollen dich warten schön;
Meine Töchter führen den nächtlichen Reihn,
Und wiegen und tanzen und singen dich ein."

Mein Vater, mein Vater, und siehst du nicht dort
Erlkönigs Töchter am düstern Ort?—
Mein Sohn, mein Sohn, ich seh' es genau:
Es scheinen die alten Weiden so grau.

„Ich liebe dich, mich reizt deine schöne Gestalt;
Und bist du nicht willig, so brauch' ich Gewalt."
Mein Vater, mein Vater, jetzt fasst er mich an!
Erlkönig hat mir ein Leids getan!—

Dem Vater grauset's, er reitet geschwind,
Er hält in Armen das ächzende Kind,
Erreicht den Hof mit Müh und Not;
In seinen Armen das Kind war tot.

10.   DER ZAUBERLEHRLING

Hat der alte Hexenmeister
Sich doch einmal wegbegeben!
Und nun sollen seine Geister
Auch nach meinem Willen leben.
Seine Wort' und Werke
Merkt' ich und den Brauch,
Und mit Geistesstärke
Tu' ich Wunder auch.

Walle! walle
Manche Strecke,
Dass, zum Zwecke,

'Sweet lad, o come and join me, do!
Such pretty games I will play with you,
On the shore gay flowers their color unfold,
My mother has many garments of gold.'

"My father, my father, and can you not hear
The promise the elf-king breathes in my ear?"
"Be quiet now, stay quiet, my child,
Night winds in withered leaves sough wild."

'Will you, sweet lad, come along with me?
My daughters shall care for you tenderly;
In the night my daughters their revelry keep,
They'll rock you and dance you and sing you to sleep.'

"My father, my father, o can you not trace
The elf-king's daughters in that gloomy place?"
"My son, my son, I see it clear
How grey the ancient willows appear."

'I love you, your comeliness charms me, my boy!
And if you're not willing, my force I'll employ.'
"O father, o father, he's grasping my arm!
Elf-king has done me a cruel harm."

The father shudders, his ride is wild,
In his arms he's holding the groaning child,
Reaches the court with toil and dread.—
The child he held in his arms was dead.

10.   THE SORCERER'S APPRENTICE

That old sorcerer has vanished
And for once has gone away!
Spirits called by him, now banished,
My commands shall soon obey.
Every step and saying
That he used, I know,
And with sprites obeying
My arts I will show.

Flow, flow onward
Stretches many
Spare not any

Wasser fliesse
Und mit reichem, vollem Schwalle
Zu dem Bade sich ergiesse.

Und nun komm, du alter Besen,
Nimm die schlechten Lumpenhüllen!
Bist schon lange Knecht gewesen:
Nun erfülle meinen Willen!
Auf zwei Beinen stehe,
Oben sei ein Kopf,
Eile nun und gehe
Mit dem Wassertopf!

Walle! walle
Manche Strecke,
Dass, zum Zwecke,
Wasser fliesse
Und mit reichem, vollem Schwalle
Zu dem Bade sich ergiesse.

Seht, er läuft zum Ufer nieder,
Wahrlich! ist schon an dem Flusse,
Und mit Blitzesschnelle wieder
Ist er hier mit raschem Gusse.
Schon zum zweiten Male!
Wie das Becken schwillt!
Wie sich jede Schale
Voll mit Wasser füllt!

Stehe! stehe!
Denn wir haben
Deiner Gaben
Vollgemessen!—
Ach, ich merk' es! Wehe! wehe!
Hab' ich doch das Wort vergessen!

Ach das Wort, worauf am Ende
Er das wird, was er gewesen.
Ach, er läuft und bringt behende!
Wärst du doch der alte Besen!
Immer neue Güsse
Bringt er schnell herein,
Ach! und hundert Flüsse
Stürzen auf mich ein.

Water rushing,
Ever streaming fully downward
Toward the pool in current gushing.

Come, old broomstick, you are needed,
Take these rags and wrap them round you!
Long my orders you have heeded,
By my wishes now I've bound you.
Have two legs and stand,
And a head for you.
Run, and in your hand
Hold a bucket too.

Flow, flow onward
Stretches many,
Spare not any
Water rushing,
Ever streaming fully downward
Toward the pool in current gushing.

See him, toward the shore he's racing!
There, he's at the stream already,
Back like lightning he is chasing,
Pouring water fast and steady.
Once again he hastens!
How the water spills,
How the water basins
Brimming full he fills!

Stop now, hear me!
Ample measure
Of your treasure
We have gotten!
Ah, I see it, dear me, dear me.
Master's word I have forgotten!

Ah, the word with which the master
Makes the broom a broom once more!
Ah, he runs and fetches faster!
Be a broomstick as before!
Ever new the torrents
That by him are fed,
Ah, a hundred currents
Pour upon my head!

Nein, nicht länger
Kann ich's lassen:
Will ihn fassen.
Das ist Tücke!
Ach! nun wird mir immer bänger!
Welche Miene! welche Blicke!

O, du Ausgeburt der Hölle!
Soll das ganze Haus ersaufen?
Seh' ich über jede Schwelle
Doch schon Wasserströme laufen.
Ein verruchter Besen,
Der nicht hören will!
Stock, der du gewesen,
Steh doch wieder still!

Willst's am Ende
Gar nicht lassen?
Will dich fassen,
Will dich halten
Und das alte Holz behende
Mit dem scharfen Beile spalten.

Seht, da kommt er schleppend wieder!
Wie ich mich nur auf dich werfe,
Gleich, o Kobold, liegst du nieder.
Krachend trifft die glatte Schärfe.
Wahrlich! brav getroffen!
Seht, er ist entzwei!
Und nun kann ich hoffen,
Und ich atme frei!

Wehe! wehe!
Beide Teile
Stehn in Eile
Schon als Knechte
Völlig fertig in die Höhe!
Helft mir, ach! ihr hohen Mächte!

Und sie laufen! Nass und nässer
Wird's im Saal und auf den Stufen:
Welch entsetzliches Gewässer!
Herr und Meister! hör' mich rufen!—
Ach, da kommt der Meister!

No, no longer
Can I please him,
I will seize him!
That is spiteful!
My misgivings grow the stronger.
What a mien, his eyes how frightful!

Brood of hell, you're not a mortal!
Shall the entire house go under?
Over threshold over portal
Streams of water rush and thunder.
Broom accurst and mean,
Who will have his will,
Stick that you have been,
Once again stand still!

Can I never,
Broom, appease you?
I will seize you,
Hold and whack you,
And your ancient wood I'll sever,
With a whetted axe I'll crack you.

He returns, more water dragging!
Now I'll throw myself upon you!
Soon, o goblin, you'll be sagging.
Crash! The sharp axe has undone you.
What a good blow, truly!
There, he's split, I see.
Hope now rises newly,
And my breathing's free.

Woe betide me!
Both halves scurry
In a hurry,
Rise like towers
There beside me.
Help me, help, eternal powers!

Off they run, till wet and wetter
Hall and steps immersed are lying.
What a flood that naught can fetter!
Lord and master, hear me crying!—
Ah, he comes excited.

Herr, die Not ist gross!
Die ich rief, die Geister,
Werd' ich nun nicht los.

„In die Ecke,
Besen! Besen!
Seid's gewesen!
Denn als Geister
Ruft euch nur, zu seinem Zwecke,
Erst hervor der alte Meister."

11.   DIE WANDELNDE GLOCKE

Es war ein Kind, das wollte nie
Zur Kirche sich bequemen,
Und Sonntags fand es stets ein Wie,
Den Weg ins Feld zu nehmen.

Die Mutter sprach: Die Glocke tönt,
Und so ist dir's befohlen,
Und hast du dich nicht hingewöhnt,
Sie kommt und wird dich holen.

Das Kind, es denkt: die Glocke hängt
Da droben auf dem Stuhle.
Schon hat's den Weg ins Feld gelenkt,
Als lief' es aus der Schule.

Die Glocke Glocke tönt nicht mehr,
Die Mutter hat gefackelt.
Doch, welch ein Schrecken! hinterher
Die Glocke kommt gewackelt.

Sie wackelt schnell, man glaubt es kaum!
Das arme Kind im Schrecken,
Es läuft, es kommt, als wie im Traum:
Die Glocke wird es decken.

Doch nimmt es richtig seinen Husch,
Und mit gewandter Schnelle
Eilt es durch Anger, Feld und Busch
Zur Kirche, zur Kapelle.

Sir, my need is sore.
Spirits that I've cited
My commands ignore.

"To the lonely
Corner, broom!
Hear your doom.
As a spirit
When he wills, your master only
Calls you, then 'tis time to hear it."

11. THE WALKING BELL

Steadfastly did a child refuse
To go to church for praying;
Sundays he always planned a ruse
And in the fields went straying.

The mother spoke: "The church bells toll,
To you 'tis so commanded,
And if to church you will not stroll,
They'll fetch you, as demanded."

The child reflects: "The bell that pealed
Is in the tower suspended,"
Then takes the path into the field,
As though school hours had ended.

"The bell, the bell has ceased to ring,
My mother has been joking.
But horrors, what a dreadful thing!
Toward me the bell is poking!"

It stomped along, though strange it seems.
In fear the child now hovered.
He runs, he comes as oft in dreams:
The bell will hold him covered!

But then he gives himself a push,
Away he nimbly lurches
And runs to field and mead and bush
To where he knows the church is.

Und jeden Sonn- und Feiertag
Gedenkt es an den Schaden,
Lässt durch den ersten Glockenschlag
Nicht in Person sich laden.

12. DER GOTT UND DIE BAJADERE

Indische Legende

Mahadöh, der Herr der Erde,
Kommt herab zum sechsten Mal,
Dass er unsersgleichen werde,
Mitzufühlen Freud' und Qual.
Er bequemt sich, hier zu wohnen,
Lässt sich alles selbst geschehn:
Soll er strafen oder schonen,
Muss er Menschen menschlich sehn.
Und hat er die Stadt sich als Wandrer betrachtet,
Die Grossen belauert, auf Kleine geachtet,
Verlässt er sie abends, um weiterzugehn.

Als er nun hinausgegangen,
Wo die letzten Häuser sind,
Sieht er, mit gemalten Wangen,
Ein verlornes schönes Kind.
„Grüss' dich, Jungfrau! "—„Dank der Ehre!
Wart', ich komme gleich hinaus."—
„Und wer bist du?"—„Bajadere,
Und dies ist der Liebe Haus."
Sie rührt sich, die Zimbeln zum Tanze zu schlagen,
Sie weiss sich so lieblich im Kreise zu tragen,
Sie neigt sich und biegt sich und reicht ihm den Strauss.

Schmeichelnd zieht sie ihn zur Schwelle,
Lebhaft ihn ins Haus hinein:
„Schöner Fremdling, lampenhelle
Soll sogleich die Hütte sein.
Bist du müd', ich will dich laben,
Lindern deiner Füsse Schmerz.
Was du willst, das sollst du haben,
Ruhe, Freuden oder Scherz."

And every Sun- and holiday
He thinks how he was spited;
The first peal drives him on his way,
He need not be invited.

12. THE GOD AND THE BAYADERE

Hindu Legend

Earth-lord Mahadeh, his portal
For the sixth time leaves again,
Coming down to be a mortal
And to feel man's joy and pain.
Deigns to share man's earthly dwelling,
Lets things happen as they can,
Blessing man or curses spelling,
He must look on man as man.
And when as a wanderer he's gazed at the city,
Observing the great and to poor showing pity,
At evening he leaves and proceeds for a span.

Now when through the outskirts faring,
Where the last small huts are piled,
There he sees a rouged and daring
Girl, a lost but pretty child.
"Greetings, maiden!" She a cheery
"Thank you" speaks, "I'll come straightway."—
"And who are you?" "Bayaderë.
In this house of love I stay."
She stirs and she dances and clashes the cymbal,
She trips in a circle, her dance is so nimble,
She curtseys and bows and holds out her bouquet.

Draws him coaxingly and sprightly
Toward the threshold, through the door:
'Handsome stranger, light shall brightly
Into all my cabin pour.
I'll revive you if you're tired,
Soothe the ache of weary feet,
Give you all that you've desired,
Rest or jest or joy complete.'

Sie lindert geschäftig geheuchelte Leiden.
Der Göttliche lächelt; er siehet mit Freuden
Durch tiefes Verderben ein menschliches Herz.

    Und er fordert Sklavendienste;
Immer heitrer wird sie nur,
Und des Mädchens frühe Künste
Werden nach und nach Natur.
Und so stellet auf die Blüte
Bald und bald die Frucht sich ein:
Ist Gehorsam im Gemüte,
Wird nicht fern die Liebe sein.
Aber, sie schärfer und schärfer zu prüfen,
Wählet der Kenner der Höhen und Tiefen
Lust und Entsetzen und grimmige Pein.

    Und er küsst die bunten Wangen,
Und sie fühlt der Liebe Qual,
Und das Mädchen steht gefangen,
Und sie weint zum erstenmal,
Sinkt zu seinen Füssen nieder,
Nicht um Wollust noch Gewinst,
Ach! und die gelenken Glieder,
Sie versagen allen Dienst.
Und so zu des Lagers vergnüglicher Feier
Bereiten den dunklen behaglichen Schleier
Die nächtlichen Stunden, das schöne Gespinst.

    Spät entschlummert unter Scherzen,
Früh erwacht nach kurzer Rast,
Findet sie an ihrem Herzen
Tot den vielgeliebten Gast.
Schreiend stürzt sie auf ihn nieder,
Aber nicht erweckt sie ihn,
Und man trägt die starren Glieder
Bald zur Flammengrube hin.
Sie höret die Priester, die Totengesänge,
Sie raset und rennet und teilet die Menge.
„Wer bist du? was drängt zu der Grube dich hin?“

    Bei der Bahre stürzt sie nieder,
Ihr Geschrei durchdringt die Luft:
„Meinen Gatten will ich wieder!

She busily soothes all the ills he's affected.
The godly one smiles; with joy he's detected
Through deep degradation a heart that can beat.

  Slavish service he required,
  But her cheer still waxes gay,
  And the arts that she's acquired
  To her natural self give way.
  For where blossoms thrive in beauty
  Soon and sooner fruits will glow;
  Where a man gives ear to duty
  Love will also not be slow.
But then, deciding more keenly to try her,
The god who knew the Lower and Higher
Chose rapture and horror and terrible woe.

  And her painted cheek he kisses,
  And she feels love's torture deep,
  And the girl is caught in blisses.
  For the first time she must weep.
  At his feet he sees her kneeling,
  Not for lust and not for gain.
  Ah, her supple limbs now reeling
  Cannot do their work again.
And so for the couch and their love's dedication
The hours of night in kind preparation
Are weaving a sheltering veil for the twain.

  Late to sleep with happy jesting,
  Soon awake from short-lived rest,
  There she finds the loved guest resting
  Cold and dead upon her breast.
  With her screams she tries to wake him,
  Ah, but she can wake him not.
  Now a rigid corpse, they take him
  To the flaming funeral lot.
She hears the priests praying, funereal chanting.
She runs through the mob with raving and ranting.
"Who are you, what drives you so close to the spot?"

  Sinking at the bier, she tarried,
  And her shrieking rent the air:
  "Give me back the man I married!

Und ich such' ihn in der Gruft.
Soll zu Asche mir zerfallen
Dieser Glieder Götterpracht?
Mein! er war es, mein vor allen!
Ach, nur e i n e süsse Nacht!"
Es singen die Priester: „Wir tragen die Alten
Nach langem Ermatten und spätem Erkalten,
Wir tragen die Jugend, noch eh' sie's gedacht.

    Höre deiner Priester Lehre:
Dieser war dein Gatte nicht.
Lebst du doch als Bajadere,
Und so hast du keine Pflicht.
Nur dem Körper folgt der Schatten
In das stille Totenreich;
Nur die Gattin folgt dem Gatten:
Das ist Pflicht und Ruhm zugleich.
Ertöne, Drommete, zu heiliger Klage!
O nehmet, ihr Götter! die Zierde der Tage,
O nehmet den Jüngling in Flammen zu euch!"

    So das Chor, das ohn' Erbarmen
Mehret ihres Herzens Not;
Und mit ausgestreckten Armen
Springt sie in den heissen Tod.
Doch der Götterjüngling hebet
Aus der Flamme sich empor,
Und in seinen Armen schwebet
Die Geliebte mit hervor.
Es freut sich die Gottheit der reuigen Sünder;
Unsterbliche heben verlorene Kinder
Mit feurigen Armen zum Himmel empor.

13.   ERGO BIBAMUS!

Hier sind wir versammelt zu löblichem Tun,
    Drum, Brüderchen, *Ergo bibamus!*
Die Gläser sie klingen, Gespräche sie ruhn,
    Beherziget *Ergo bibamus!*
Das heisst noch ein altes, ein tüchtiges Wort,

In the grave I'll seek him there.
Shall that godlike form, decaying,
Turn to ash in fire's blight?
He was mine alone, though staying
With me but one raptured night."
The priests are heard chanting: "We carry the old ones
And those long fatigued, the belatedly cold ones,
We carry the young while their life was still bright."

    "Hear your priests their counsel saying:
This man was not wed to you.
You, the bayaderë playing,
Have no duty that is true.
Shades alone to death's still hollow
Can attend the mortal frame;
Wives alone their husbands follow:
That is duty, that is fame.
Sound clearly, o trumpet, for solemnest mourning,
Now take him, o gods, our age once adorning,
O take on your bosom the youth from the flame!"

    So the choir, entreaties spurning,
Makes her sorrow mount still higher;
She, her arms to heaven upturning,
Leaps into the funeral pyre.
But the godly youth arises
From the brilliant flaming light,
And the girl he loves and prizes
In his arm takes upward flight.
The godhead rejoices in sinners' contrition;
Immortals take children once meant for perdition
In fiery embrace to a heaven of delight.

13. ERGO BIBAMUS

Here now we're assembled for worthy ado,
So brothers, an *Ergo bibamus*!
The glasses are clinking, and words are but few,
Remember then, *Ergo bibamus*!
To us it's a phrase that is age-old and sound,

Es passet zum ersten und passet so fort,
Und schallet ein Echo vom festlichen Ort,
    Ein herrliches *Ergo bibamus!*

Ich hatte mein freundliches Liebchen gesehn,
    Da dacht' ich mir: *Ergo bibamus!*
Und nahte mich freundlich, da liess sie mich stehn,
    Ich half mir und dachte: *Bibamus!*
Und wenn sie versöhnet euch herzet und küsst,
Und wenn ihr das Herzen und Küssen vermisst,
So bleibet nur, bis ihr was Besseres wisst,
    Beim tröstlichen *Ergo bibamus!*

Mich ruft mein Geschick von den Freunden hinweg:
    Ihr redlichen! *Ergo bibamus!*
Ich scheide von hinnen mit leichtem Gepäck,
    Drum doppeltes *Ergo bibamus!*
Und was auch der Filz von dem Leibe sich schmorgt,
So bleibt für den Heitren doch immer gesorgt,
Weil immer dem Frohen der Fröhliche borgt:
    Drum, Brüderchen, *Ergo bibamus!*

Was sollen wir sagen zum heutigen Tag?
    Ich dächte nur: *Ergo bibamus!*
Er ist nun einmal von besonderem Schlag,
    Drum immer aufs neue: *Bibamus!*
Er führet die Freude durchs offene Tor,
Es glänzen die Wolken, es teilt sich der Flor,
Da leuchtet ein Bildchen, ein göttliches, vor!
    Wir klingen und singen: *Bibamus!*

14. ERINNERUNG

    Willst du immer weiter schweifen?
Sieh, das Gute liegt so nah.
Lerne nur das Glück ergreifen,
Denn das Glück ist immer da.

15. NÄHE DES GELIEBTEN

Ich denke dein, wenn mir der Sonne Schimmer
    Vom Meere strahlt;

'Twas fitting at first, and still fitting it's found,
And from our wassailing an echo goes round,
A glorious *Ergo bibamus.*

I'd seen my dear love who had been debonair,
I said to me: *Ergo bibamus!*
With smiles I approached, but she gave me the air,
I cheered myself, thinking: *Bibamus!*
And when she's appeased and will fondle and kiss,
And when her embraces and kisses you miss,
Remain, till you hit on some happier bliss,
With comforting *Ergo bibamus!*

From friendships my destiny calls me away:
Good fellows, an *Ergo bibamus!*
With lightest belongings farewell I will say,
So double our *Ergo bibamus!*
However the miser may stint with his fare,
The light-hearted always are sure of their share,
For always the gay lend to those free of care;
So, brothers, sing *Ergo bibamus!*

What words on this noteworthy day shall we find?
My only thought: *Ergo bibamus!*
It happens to be one unique of its kind,
So over and over; *Bibamus!*
It leads us in joy through the wide-open door,
The clouds are resplendent, the haze is no more;
A vision, a godly one, beams to the fore!
We clink and keep singing: *Bibamus!*

14. RECOLLECTION

Onward would you roam forever?
See, the good is lying here.
Seize it with a bold endeavor,
Happiness is always near.

15. THE BELOVED IS NEAR

I think of you, dear, when with sunlight's beaming
The sea is bright;

Ich denke dein, wenn sich des Mondes Flimmer
　　In Quellen malt.

Ich sehe dich, wenn auf dem fernen Wege
　　Der Staub sich hebt;
In tiefer Nacht, wenn auf dem schmalen Stege
　　Der Wandrer bebt.

Ich höre dich, wenn dort mit dumpfem Rauschen
　　Die Welle steigt;
Im stillen Haine geh' ich oft zu lauschen,
　　Wenn alles schweigt.

Ich bin bei dir, du seist auch noch so ferne,
　　Du bist mir nah!
Die Sonne sinkt, bald leuchten mir die Sterne.
　　O wärst du da!

16. MEERES STILLE

Tiefe Stille herrscht im Wasser,
Ohne Regung ruht das Meer,
Und bekümmert sieht der Schiffer
Glatte Fläche rings umher.
Keine Luft von keiner Seite!
Todesstille fürchterlich!
In der ungeheuren Weite
Reget keine Welle sich.

17. GLÜCKLICHE FAHRT

Die Nebel zerreissen,
Der Himmel ist helle,
Und Äolus löset
Das ängstliche Band.
Es säuseln die Winde,
Es rührt sich der Schiffer.
Geschwinde! Geschwinde!
Es teilt sich die Welle,
Es naht sich die Ferne;
Schon seh' ich das Land!

I think of you when rays of moonlight gleaming
    Paint fountains white.

I see you when upon the distant ridges
    The dust-cloud plays;
In nighttime's darkness, when on narrow bridges
    The traveler sways.

I hear you when with roaring waves that glisten
    The tide has rushed;
In quiet grove I often go to listen
    When all is hushed.

I am with you, however far you're going,
    Still you are near!
The sun has set, the stars will soon be glowing.
    Would you were here!

16. CALM AT SEA

Deepest quiet rules the water,
And the main rests silently,
While concerned the sailor faces
Round about unruffled sea.
Nowhere is a breeze in motion!
Silence awesome as the grave!
In the vast expanse of ocean
Motionless is every wave.

17. HAPPY VOYAGE

The fog-banks are scattered
And heaven is radiant,
While Aeolus looses
The troublesome bond.
The gentle winds murmur,
The skipper is active
O hurry, o hurry!
The wave is divided,
The distance is nearer,
And soon I see land.

18. SCHÄFERS KLAGELIED

Da droben auf jenem Berge,
Da steh' ich tausendmal,
An meinem Stabe gebogen,
Und schaue hinab in das Tal.

Dann folg' ich der weidenden Herde,
Mein Hündchen bewahret mir sie.
Ich bin herunter gekommen
Und weiss doch selber nicht wie.

Da stehet von schönen Blumen
Die ganze Wiese so voll.
Ich breche sie, ohne zu wissen,
Wem ich sie geben soll.

Und Regen, Sturm und Gewitter
Verpass' ich unter dem Baum.
Die Türe dort bleibet verschlossen;
Doch alles ist leider ein Traum.

Es stehet ein Regenbogen
Wohl über jenem Haus!
Sie aber ist weggezogen,
Und weit in das Land hinaus.

Hinaus in das Land und weiter,
Vielleicht gar über die See.
Vorüber, ihr Schafe, vorüber!
Dem Schäfer ist gar so weh.

19. DIE SPRÖDE

An dem reinsten Frühlingsmorgen
Ging die Schäferin und sang,
Jung und schön und ohne Sorgen,
Dass es durch die Felder klang,
So la la! le ral-la!

Thyrsis bot ihr für ein Mäulchen
Zwei, drei Schäfchen gleich am Ort.
Schalkhaft blickte sie ein Weilchen,

18. SHEPHERD'S PLAINT

Aloft to the hilltop yonder
A thousand times I go,
Upon my staff supported,
I gaze at the valley below.

The pasturing sheep I follow,
My dog, he watches them well,
And then I came down from the hilltop,
But how, even I cannot tell.

With beautiful flowers the meadow
Is blossoming bright and gay.
I pick them, but never knowing
To whom I should give them away.

The time of rainstorm and shower
Under the tree I pass.
The door nearby is not open;
But all is a dream, alas!

Over that house a rainbow
I see is arching its band.
But she has long departed
And gone far over the land.

Across the land and still further,
Over the sea, who would know?
Move on, you sheep in the pasture!
The shepherd is full of woe.

19. THE COY GIRL

In the dawn of spring, the rarest,
Shepherdess went forth and sang,
Carefree, young, and of the fairest,
Through the fields her singing rang,
So la la! lay ral-la!

Thyrsis for a kiss would proffer
Two, three lambs without delay.
Roguishly she heard the offer,

Doch sie sang und lachte fort,
So la la! le ral-la!

Und ein andrer bot ihr Bänder,
Und der dritte bot sein Herz.
Doch sie trieb mit Herz und Bändern
So wie mit den Lämmern Scherz,
Nur la la! le ral-la!

20. MAILIED

Zwischen Weizen und Korn,
Zwischen Hecken und Dorn,
Zwischen Bäumen und Gras,
Wo geht's Liebchen?
Sag' mir das!

Fand mein Holdchen
Nicht daheim:
Muss das Goldchen
Draussen sein.
Grünt und blühet
Schön der Mai,
Liebchen ziehet
Froh und frei.

An dem Felsen beim Fluss,
Wo sie reichte den Kuss,
Jenen ersten im Gras,
Seh' ich etwas!
Ist sie das?

21. NATUR UND KUNST

Natur und Kunst, sie scheinen sich zu fliehen
Und haben sich, eh' man es denkt, gefunden;
Der Widerwille ist auch mir verschwunden,
Und beide scheinen gleich mich anzuziehen.

Sang and rocked with laughter gay,
So la la! Lay ral-la!

And another offered ribbons,
And a third his heart, poor boy!
But the maid with heart and ribbons
As with lambs would only toy,
Ah la la! Lay ral-la!

20. SONG OF MAY

Midst the wheat and the corn,
Midst the hedges and thorn,
Midst the grasses and trees,
Where is my lover?
Tell me, please!

If my little one
Lost her way,
Then my pretty one
Still must stray.
Greening brightly,
May blooms fair;
She trips lightly,
Free of care.

At the rock by the brook,
Where she gave what I took:
That first kiss in the lea—
What's that I see?
Is it she?

21. NATURE AND ART

Nature and Art, it seems to us, diverge,
But soon, before we know it, are united;
I find myself by both alike delighted,
And both attract me with magnetic urge.

Es gilt wohl nur ein redliches Bemühen!
Und wenn wir erst in abgemess'nen Stunden
Mit Geist und Fleiss uns an die Kunst gebunden,
Mag frei Natur im Herzen wieder glühen.

So ist's mit aller Bildung auch beschaffen.
Vergebens werden ungebundne Geister
Nach der Vollendung reiner Höhe streben.

Wer Grosses will, muss sich zusammenraffen.
In der Beschränkung zeigt sich erst der Meister,
Und das Gesetz nur kann uns Freiheit geben.

It is but honest striving we require!
And only after long and measured hours,
Given to Art with all our spirit's powers
Can Nature in our hearts again catch fire.

Man's life and growth all take the self-same courses.
In vain will minds with unchained inspiration
Aspire to reach the heights of pure perfection.

Who would achieve, he must command his forces.
A master shows his powers in limitation,
And freedom follows only law's direction.

CHAPTER VII. ITALY

1. RÖMISCHE ELEGIEN I.

Saget, Steine, mir an, o sprecht, ihr hohen Paläste!
   Strassen, redet ein Wort! Genius, regst du dich nicht?
Ja, es ist alles beseelt in deinen heiligen Mauern,
   Ewige Roma; nur mir schweiget noch alles so still.
O, wer flüstert mir zu, an welchem Fenster erblick' ich
   Einst das holde Geschöpf, das mich versengend erquickt?
Ahn' ich die Wege noch nicht, durch die ich immer und immer,
   Zu ihr und von ihr zu gehn, opfre die köstliche Zeit?
Noch betracht' ich Kirch' und Palast, Ruinen und Säulen,
   Wie ein bedächtiger Mann schicklich die Reise benutzt.
Doch bald ist es vorbei; dann wird ein einziger Tempel,
   Amors Tempel, nur sein, der den Geweihten empfängt.
Eine Welt zwar bist du, o Rom; doch ohne die Liebe
   Wäre die Welt nicht die Welt, wäre denn Rom auch nicht Rom.

2. RÖMISCHE ELEGIEN V.

Froh empfind' ich mich nun auf klassischem Boden begeistert,
   Vor- und Mitwelt spricht lauter und reizender mir.
Hier befolg' ich den Rat, durchblättre die Werke der Alten
   Mit geschäftiger Hand, täglich mit neuem Genuss.
Aber die Nächte hindurch hält Amor mich anders beschäftigt;
   Werd' ich auch halb nur gelehrt, bin ich doch doppelt beglückt.
Und belehr' ich mich nicht, indem ich des lieblichen Busens
   Formen spähe, die Hand leite die Hüften hinab?
Dann versteh' ich den Marmor erst recht: ich denk' und vergleiche,
   Sehe mit fühlendem Aug', fühle mit sehender Hand.
Raubt die Liebste denn gleich mir einige Stunden des Tages,
   Gibt sie Stunden der Nacht mir zur Entschädigung hin.
Wird doch nicht immer geküsst, es wird vernünftig gesprochen;
   Überfällt sie der Schlaf, lieg' ich und denke mir viel.
Oftmals hab' ich auch schon in ihren Armen gedichtet
   Und des Hexameters Mass leise mit fingernder Hand
Ihr auf den Rücken gezählt. Sie atmet in lieblichem Schlummer,
   Und es durchglühet ihr Hauch mir bis ins Tiefste die Brust.
Amor schüret die Lamp' indes und denket der Zeiten,
   Da er den nämlichen Dienst seinen Triumvirn getan.

1. ROMAN ELEGIES I.

Stones, announce it to me, o speak, you palaces lofty!
　　Streets, o utter a word! Genius, will you not stir?
Every object has life within your walls that are holy,
　　Rome eternal, and yet all is silent for me.
Who will whisper to me, behind which window will beckon
　　That sweet creature some day, quickening me with her fire?
Do I by now not sense the paths that ever and ever
　　To her and from her I walked, wasting my costliest time?
Yet I scan each palace and church, the ruins and columns,
　　As a sensible man properly uses his stay.
Soon though all will be gone, and then one singular temple,
　　Cupid's alone, will remain, welcoming his devotee.
Rome, you are truly a world, but without a love to enhance it
　　Not would the world be the world, Rome no longer be Rome.

2. ROMAN ELEGIES V.

Happily now on classical soil I feel inspiration;
　　Yesteryear's world and today's charm me more audibly now.
Here I obey the advice and page through the works of the
　　　ancients
With an industrious hand, daily with pleasure renewed.
But through the still of the night I am otherwise busied by Cupid;
　　Though I grow learned but half, twofold my happiness beams.
Am I not teaching myself by spying the ravishing bosom's
　　Forms, and by guiding my hand down from the round of the
　　　hips?
Then I fathom the marble at last; I think and compare it,
　　See with a feeling eye, feel with a seeing hand.
Though my lover may rob me of several hours of the daytime,
　　Hours of the night she gives—compensation enough.
True, not always we kiss, we also have sensible converse;
　　When she is taken by sleep, many my thoughts as I lie.
Often too in her arms I've lain composing a poem,
　　Counting hexameters out, softly with fingering hand
Tapping her back. She breathes in quiet, ravishing slumber,
　　And her breath glows warm, touching the depth of my heart.
Meanwhile Cupid nurses the lamp, recalling the ages
　　When his triumvirs he gave similar service of love.

3. RÖMISCHE ELEGIEN VII.

O wie fühl' ich in Rom mich so froh, gedenk' ich der Zeiten,
    Da mich ein graulicher Tag hinten im Norden umfing,
Trübe der Himmel und schwer auf meine Scheitel sich senkte,
    Farb- und gestaltlos die Welt um den Ermatteten lag,
Und ich über mein Ich, des unbefriedigten Geistes
    Düstre Wege zu spähn, still in Betrachtung versank.
Nun umleuchtet der Glanz des helleren Äthers die Stirne,
    Phöbus rufet, der Gott, Formen und Farben hervor.
Sternhell glänzet die Nacht, sie klingt von weichen Gesängen,
    Und mir leuchtet der Mond heller als nordischer Tag.
Welche Seligkeit ward mir Sterblichem! Träum' ich? Empfänget
    Dein ambrosisches Haus, Jupiter Vater, den Gast?
Ach! hier lieg' ich, und strecke nach deinen Knien die Hände
    Flehend aus. O vernimm, Jupiter Xenius, mich!
Wie ich hereingekommen, ich kann's nicht sagen: es fasste
    Hebe den Wandrer und zog mich in die Hallen heran.
Hast du ihr einen Heroen heraufzuführen geboten?
    Irrte die Schöne? Vergib! Lass mir des Irrtums Gewinn!
Deine Tochter Fortuna, sie auch! Die herrlichsten Gaben
    Teilt als ein Mädchen sie aus, wie es die Laune gebeut.
Bist du der wirtliche Gott? O dann so verstosse den Gastfreund
    Nicht von deinem Olymp wieder zur Erde hinab!
„Dichter! wohin versteigest du dich?"—Vergib mir; der hohe
    Kapitolinische Berg ist dir ein zweiter Olymp.
Dulde mich, Jupiter, hier, und Hermes führe mich später,
    Cestius' Mal vorbei, leise zum Orkus hinab.

4. RÖMISCHE ELEGIEN XIV.

Zünde mir Licht an, Knabe!—„Noch ist es hell. Ihr verzehret
    Öl und Docht nur umsonst. Schliesset die Läden doch nicht!
Hinter die Häuser entwich, nicht hinter den Berg, uns die Sonne!
    Ein halb Stündchen noch währt's bis zum Geläute der Nacht."
Unglückseliger! geh und gehorch'! Mein Mädchen erwart' ich;
    Tröste mich, Lämpchen, indes, lieblicher Bote der Nacht!

3. ROMAN ELEGIES VII.

O how happy I feel in Rome recalling the hours
  When a grey, chilly day held me confined in the North,
Cloudy the skies and heavy that lowered their darkness upon me,
  Colorless, formless the world round my weariness lay,
And I quietly fell to contemplating my ego,
  Wishing to find dark ways taken by sad discontent.
Now my brow is enveloped by ether that's radiantly brighter;
  Phoebus Apollo, the god, calls forth colors and forms.
Star-lit sparkles the night, it rings with soft-throated singing,
  Clear is the moon for me, lighter than day in the North.
O what bliss for a mortal like me! Am I dreaming? O father,
  Has thy ambrosial house, Jupiter, welcomed the guest?
Here I lie and seek thy knees with hands that implore thee.
  O give ear to my plea, Jupiter Xenius, hear!
How I entered I cannot say; there came to the wanderer
  Hebe and held me tight, drew me into the halls.
Hast thou sent her commands to bring to thy precincts a hero?
  Could fair Hebe have erred? Pardon! Let *me* have the gain!
She too, Fortune, thy daughter, dispenses the loveliest bounties,
  Taking the form of a girl, guided by a caprice.
Hospitable art thou? O then reject not the guest-friend
  On thy Olympus, and turn me not earthward again!
"Poet, you're soaring too high in the clouds!" Forgive me, the lofty
  Capitoline, it too is an Olympus for thee.
Jupiter, bear with me here, and, Hermes, later escort me,
  Passing Cestius' tomb, gently to Orcus' domain.

4. ROMAN ELEGIES XIV.

Kindle a light, o lad!—"The day is still bright. You're consuming
  Oil and wick but in vain. Leave the shutters untouched!
See, the sun is still over the hill, 'tis the houses that shade it!
  One half-hour more, then the curfew will ring."
Wretch unfortunate, go and obey! I wait for my lover;
  Lamp, console me the while, messenger sweet of the night!

5. EPIGRAMME VENEDIG 1790. III.

Klein ist unter den Fürsten Germaniens freilich der meine,
    Kurz und schmal ist sein Land, mässig nur, was er vermag.
Aber so wende nach innen, so wende nach aussen die Kräfte
    Jeder: da wär's ein Fest, Deutscher mit Deutschen zu sein.
Doch was priesest du Ihn, den Taten und Werke verkünden?
    Und bestochen erschien' deine Verehrung vielleicht;
Denn mir hat er gegeben, was Grosse selten gewähren:
    Neigung, Musse, Vertraun, Felder und Garten und Haus.
Niemand braucht' ich zu danken als Ihm, und manches bedurft'
    ich,
    Der ich mich auf den Erwerb schlecht, als ein Dichter, ver-
    stand.
Hat mich Europa gelobt, was hat mir Europa gegeben?
    Nichts! Ich habe, wie schwer! meine Gedichte bezahlt.
Deutschland ahmte mich nach, und Frankreich mochte mich
    lesen.
    England! freundlich empfingst du den zerrütteten Gast.
Doch was fördert es mich, dass auch sogar der Chinese
    Malet, mit ängstlicher Hand, Werthern und Lotten auf Glas?
Niemals frug ein Kaiser nach mir, es hat sich kein König
    Um mich bekümmert, und Er war mir August und Mäcen.

6. KOPHTISCHES LIED

    Lasset Gelehrte sich zanken und streiten,
Streng und bedächtig die Lehrer auch sein!
Alle die Weisesten aller der Zeiten
Lächeln und winken und stimmen mit ein:
Töricht, auf Bessrung der Toren zu harren!
Kinder der Klugheit, o habet die Narren
Eben zum Narren auch, wie sich's gehört!

    Merlin der Alte, im leuchtenden Grabe,
Wo ich als Jüngling gesprochen ihn habe,
Hat mich mit ähnlicher Antwort belehrt:
Töricht, auf Bessrung der Toren zu harren!
Kinder der Klugheit, o habet die Narren
Eben zum Narren auch, wie sich's gehört!

5. VENETIAN EPIGRAM III.

Small indeed is my prince among all Germany's princes,
 Slender and narrow his land, moderate what he can do.
But if each ruler employed, at home and elsewhere, his powers
 Equally well: 'Twere a joy German with Germans to be.
Yet why praise this prince whom his deeds and his works are
  proclaiming?
 Yes, your homage might seem bribed by his favors perhaps;
For he has given to me what the powerful seldom will grant us:
 Leisure, affection, and trust, fields and a garden and house.
No one I needed to thank but himself, and needs I had many,
 Since I lacked power to earn, being a poet, you see.
Europe has praised me, indeed, but what did I profit from
  Europe?
Nothing! How dearly I've paid, paid for the poems I wrote!
Germany followed my lead and France has read me with pleasure.
 England, you greeted me well, welcomed the guest, all distraught.
Yet what gain have I won when even the painters of China
 Paint with scrupulous hand Werther and Lottë on glass?
Never has Emperor asked after me, nor King thought about me.
 He was Augustus to me, he my Maecenas as well.

6. COPHTIC SONG I

Leave the disputing and quarrels to sages,
Teachers, deliberate rigorously!
All of the wisest in all of the ages
Beckon and smile in agreement with me:
Foolish to wait till the fools become witty!
Children of prudence, for fools there's no pity
If you make fools of them, that is their due!

Merlin, the old, in his shining tomb resting,
Where I addressed him when young I went questing,
Taught me an answer that's similar too:
Foolish to wait till the fools become witty!
Children of prudence, for fools there's no pity
If you make fools of them, that is their due!

Und auf den Höhen der indischen Lüfte
Und in den Tiefen der ägyptischen Grüfte
Hab' ich das heilige Wort nur gehört:
Töricht, auf Bessrung der Toren zu harren!
Kinder der Klugheit, o habet die Narren
Eben zum Narren auch, wie sich's gehört.

7. EIN ANDERES

Geh! gehorche meinen Winken,
Nutze deine jungen Tage,
Lerne zeitig klüger sein!
Auf des Glückes grosser Wage
Steht die Zunge selten ein:
Du musst steigen oder sinken,
Du musst herrschen und gewinnen,
Oder dienen und verlieren,
Leiden oder triumphieren,
Amboss oder Hammer sein.

When atop India's summits high-piled,
Or in deep caverns of Egypt I whiled,
Always I've heard the words sacred and true:
Foolish to wait till the fools become witty!
Children of prudence, for fools there's no pity
If you make fools of them, that is their due!

7. COPHTIC SONG II

Go, obey my nod and calling,
Put to use your youthful talents,
Learn more prudence presently!
Fortune's mighty scale and balance
Move their index ceaselessly.
You must rise or else be falling,
You must rule and be a winner,
Or a slave who always loses.
You must win or suffer bruises,
Sledge or anvil you must be.

CHAPTER VIII.   WEST-EASTERLY DIVAN

1. WER DAS DICHTEN WILL VERSTEHEN

Wer das Dichten will verstehen,
Muss ins Land der Dichtung gehen;
Wer den Dichter will verstehen,
Muss in Dichters Lande gehen.

2. HEGIRE

Nord und West und Süd zersplittern,
Throne bersten, Reiche zittern:
Flüchte du, im reinen Osten
Patriarchenluft zu kosten!
Unter Lieben, Trinken, Singen
Soll dich Chisers Quell verjüngen.

Dort, im Reinen und im Rechten
Will ich menschlichen Geschlechten
In des Ursprungs Tiefe dringen,
Wo sie noch von Gott empfingen
Himmelslehr' in Erdesprachen
Und sich nicht den Kopf zerbrachen.

Wo sich Väter hoch verehrten,
Jeden fremden Dienst verwehrten;
Will mich freun der Jugendschranke:
Glaube weit, eng der Gedanke,
Wie das Wort so wichtig dort war,
Weil es ein gesprochen Wort war.

Will mich unter Hirten mischen,
An Oasen mich erfrischen,
Wenn mit Karawanen wandle,
Shawl, Kaffee und Moschus handle;
Jeden Pfad will ich betreten
Von der Wüste zu den Städten.

Bösen Felsweg auf und nieder
Trösten, Hafis, deine Lieder,
Wenn der Führer mit Entzücken
Von des Maultiers hohem Rücken
Singt, die Sterne zu erwecken
Und die Räuber zu erschrecken.

1. POETRY YOU'D UNDERSTAND?

Poetry you'd understand?
Then go out and seek its land;
Poets you would understand?
Then go seek the poet's land.

2. HEGIRA

North, West, South in fragments break,
Thrones are bursting, empires quake:
Seek the unsullied East, for there
You'll sense patriarchal air!
There you'll love and drink and sing,
Growing young at Chiser's spring.

There in purity and right,
In the depths I'll seek for light
On the origins of mortals,
Where they learned at God's own portals
Plain in words each heavenly fact,
Letting not their brains be racked.

Patriarchs revered their brothers
But refused to work for others;
Primitive's my frame of mind!
Faith was much and thought confined,
Where the word was of the essence,
Spoken in the hearer's presence.

To the shepherds I'll betake me,
Each oasis will remake me,
When in caravans I dwell,
Shawl and musk and coffee sell;
I will travel every byway
From the desert to the highway.

If the rocky grades engage me,
Your songs, Hafis, will assuage me,
When the leader of the pack,
Joyful from the mule's high back
Sings to bid the stars awake
And to make the robbers quake.

Will in Bädern und in Schenken,
Heil'ger Hafis, dein gedenken,
Wenn den Schleier Liebchen lüftet,
Schüttelnd Ambralocken düftet.
Ja, des Dichters Liebeflüstern
Mache selbst die Huris lüstern.

Wolltet ihr ihm dies beneiden
Oder etwa gar verleiden,
Wisset nur, dass Dichterworte
Um des Paradieses Pforte
Immer leise klopfend schweben,
Sich erbittend ew'ges Leben.

3.- 5. TALISMANE

3.   Gottes ist der Orient!
Gottes ist der Okzident!
Nord- und südliches Gelände
Ruht im Frieden seiner Hände.

* * *

4.   Mich verwirren will das Irren;
Doch du weisst mich zu entwirren.
Wenn ich handle, wenn ich dichte,
Gib du meinem Weg die Richte!

* * *

5.   Im Atemholen sind zweierlei Gnaden:
Die Luft einziehn, sich ihrer entladen.
Jenes bedrängt, dieses erfrischt;
So wunderbar ist das Leben gemischt.
Du danke Gott, wenn er dich presst,
Und dank' ihm, wenn er dich wieder entlässt.

6. SELIGE SEHNSUCHT

Sagt es niemand, nur den Weisen,
Weil die Menge gleich verhöhnet:
Das Lebend'ge will ich preisen,
Das nach Flammentod sich sehnet.

In the baths and taverns too,
Hafis, I will think of you
When her veil my loved one lifts,
Scent from shaken tresses drifts.
Yes, the poet's love sighs must
Fill the houris too with lust.

If you'd envy him his doing
Or attempt to rouse his ruing,
Poet's words, you will discover,
Always tapping gently, hover
Over heaven's very portal,
Seeking life that is immortal.

3.- 5. TALISMANS

3.   God is of the East possessed!
God is ruler of the West!
Northland, southland, each direction
Rests beneath His calm protection.

*   *   *

4.   All my erring would confuse me,
But you come to disabuse me.
As I write and live and do,
Guide me well, I beg of you!

*   *   *

5.   Two boons in breathing I know about:
Inhaling the air and breathing it out.
The former oppresses, the latter refreshes;
So wondrous are life's commingled meshes.
You, thank the Lord whenever He grieves you,
And thank Him also when He relieves you.

6. BLISSFUL YEARNING

Tell it only to the sages,
Since the rabble likes to spurn:
Life I'd praise in all its stages
That for death in fire would yearn.

In der Liebesnächte Kühlung,
Die dich zeugte, wo du zeugtest,
Überfällt dich fremde Fühlung,
Wenn die stille Kerze leuchtet.

Nicht mehr bleibest du umfangen
In der Finsternis Beschattung,
Und dich reisset neu Verlangen
Auf zu höherer Begattung.

Keine Ferne macht dich schwierig,
Kommst geflogen und gebannt,
Und zuletzt, des Lichts begierig,
Bist du Schmetterling verbrannt.

Und so lang' du das nicht hast,
Dieses: Stirb und werde!
Bist du nur ein trüber Gast
Auf der dunklen Erde.

7.- 9. BUCH DER SPRÜCHE

7.   Wenn man auch nach Mecca triebe
Christus Esel, würd' er nicht
Dadurch besser abgericht,
Sondern stets ein Esel bliebe.

* * *

8.   „Du hast gar vielen nicht gedankt,
Die dir so manches Gute gegeben!"
Darüber bin ich nicht erkrankt—
Ihre Gaben mir im Herzen leben.

* * *

9.   Wisse, dass mir sehr missfällt,
Wenn so viele singen und reden!
Wer treibt die Dichtkunst aus der Welt?
Die Poeten!

10. AN VOLLEN BÜSCHELZWEIGEN

An vollen Büschelzweigen,
Geliebte, sieh nur hin!

In the chilly nights of love
You, begotten, then begetting,
Found strange feelings toward you move,
Where a quiet light is fretting.

Darkness now no longer bears you
In its gloomy obscuration,
And a new desire tears you
Up to nobler procreation.

By the distance never daunted,
You come flying, spellbound, turned
To the light that you have wanted,
Till you, moth, at last are burned.

And until with this you're blessed:
"Die, then live all over!"
You are but a wretched guest
In this world—a rover.

7.- 9. BOOK OF SAYINGS

7. If the ass that bore the Savior
   Were dispatched to Mecca, he
   Would not change but still would be
   Just an ass in his behavior.
   *   *   *
8. "To many you owe a 'thank you' still
   For frequent good that they've been giving!"
   Because of that I've not grown ill—
   Within my heart their gifts are living.
   *   *   *
9. I'll not call it cause for mirth
   When so many sing and patter.
   What's driving poetry from the earth?
                    Poets' chatter!

10. LET BRANCHES FULL AND SWELLING

Let branches full and swelling,
My love, by you be seen!

Lass dir die Früchte zeigen,
Umschalet stachlig grün.

Sie hängen längst geballet,
Still, unbekannt mit sich;
Ein Ast, der schaukelnd wallet,
Wiegt sie geduldiglich.

Doch immer reift von innen
Und schwillt der braune Kern;
Er möchte Luft gewinnen
Und säh' die Sonne gern.

Die Schale platzt, und nieder
Macht er sich freudig los;
So fallen meine Lieder
Gehäuft in deinen Schoss.

11. SULEIKA

In tausend Formen magst du dich verstecken,
Doch, Allerliebste, gleich erkenn' ich dich;
Du magst mit Zauberschleiern dich bedecken,
Allgegenwärt'ge, gleich erkenn' ich dich.

An der Zypresse reinstem, jungem Streben,
Allschöngewachs'ne, gleich erkenn' ich dich;
In des Kanales reinem Wellenleben,
Allschmeichelhafte, wohl erkenn' ich dich.

Wenn steigend sich der Wasserstrahl entfaltet,
Allspielende, wie froh erkenn' ich dich;
Wenn Wolke sich gestaltend umgestaltet,
Allmannigfalt'ge, dort erkenn' ich dich.

An des geblümten Schleiers Wiesenteppich,
Allbuntbesternte, schön erkenn' ich dich;
Und greift umher ein tausendarm'ger Eppich,
O Allumklammernde, da kenn' ich dich.

Wenn am Gebirg der Morgen sich entzündet,
Gleich, Allerheiternde, begrüss' ich dich;
Dann über mir der Himmel rein sich rundet,
Allherzerweiternde, dann atm' ich dich.

Observe the fruits indwelling,
Encased in prickly green.

They hang asleep in covers
Long since, all unaware;
A branch that sways and hovers
Rocks them with patient care.

But in them still maturing
The swelling seed is browned;
It craves the air alluring,
And sunlight all around.

The ripened husk starts popping,
Seeds gladly leave their nest;
Just so my songs come dropping,
Upon your lap to rest.

11. SULEIKA

Although in countless forms you may be shrouded,
I know you, All-belovéd, all the while;
Although in magic veils you may be clouded,
All-present one, I know you all the while.

In cypress trees' most pure and youthful striving,
All-stateliest, I know you all the while;
And in the channel waves' pure, limpid driving
I know you, All-caressing, all the while.

And when the fountain sends its column looping,
All-playful one, in joy I know you then;
When cloud-banks change their contour in regrouping,
All-manifold one, there I know you then.

And on the meadow's veil-like rug of flowers,
All-starred in color, fair I know you there;
When myriad-arméd ivy shapes its bowers,
O All-embracing, how I know you then.

When on the hill the morning light has flamed,
All-gladdener, my greetings go to you;
When over me pure skies their arch have framed,
All-heart-expander, then I breathe but you.

Was ich mit äusserm Sinn, mit innerm kenne,
Du Allbelehrende, kenn' ich durch dich;
Und wenn ich Allahs Namenhundert nenne,
Mit jedem klingt ein Name nach für dich.

12. SOLLT' ICH NICHT—

Sollt' ich nicht ein Gleichnis brauchen,
Wie es mir beliebt,
Da uns Gott des Lebens Gleichnis
In der Mücke gibt?

Sollt' ich nicht ein Gleichnis brauchen,
Wie es mir beliebt,
Da mir Gott in Liebchens Augen
Sich im Gleichnis gibt?

What I with outward, inward sense acquired,
All-teaching teacher, I have learned from you;
When calling Allah's hundred names inspired,
There verberates with each a name for you.

12. WHY SHOULD—

Why should symbol then be banished
If I'm fond of that?
For life's symbol God has shown us
In the lowly gnat.

Why should symbol then be banished
If its use I prize,
When God's very symbol meets me
In my loved one's eyes?

CHAPTER IX. OLD AGE

1. EPILOG ZU SCHILLERS GLOCKE

Freude dieser Stadt bedeute,
Friede sei ihr erst Geläute!

Und so geschah's! Dem friedenreichen Klange
Bewegte sich das Land, und segenbar
Ein frisches Glück erschien: im Hochgesange
Begrüssten wir das junge Fürstenpaar,
Im Vollgewühl, in lebensregem Drange
Vermischte sich die tät'ge Völkerschar,
Und festlich ward an die geschmückten Stufen
D i e H u l d i g u n g d e r K ü n s t e vorgerufen.

Da hör' ich schreckhaft mitternächt'ges Läuten,
Das dumpf und schwer die Trauertöne schwellt.
Ist's möglich? Soll es unsern Freund bedeuten,
An den sich jeder Wunsch geklammert hält?
Den Lebenswürd'gen soll der Tod erbeuten?
Ach! wie verwirrt solch ein Verlust die Welt!
Ach! was zerstört ein solcher Riss den Seinen!
Nun weint die Welt, und sollten wir nicht weinen?

Denn er war unser! Wie bequem gesellig
Den hohen Mann der gute Tag gezeigt,
Wie bald sein Ernst, anschliessend, wohlgefällig,
Zur Wechselrede heiter sich geneigt,
Bald raschgewandt, geistreich und sicherstellig
Der Lebensplane tiefen Sinn erzeugt
Und fruchtbar sich in Rat und Tat ergossen:
Das haben wir erfahren und genossen.

Denn er war unser! Mag das stolze Wort
Den lauten Schmerz gewaltig übertönen!
Er mochte sich bei uns, im sichern Port,
Nach wildem Sturm zum Dauernden gewöhnen.
Indessen schritt sein Geist gewaltig fort
Ins Ewige des Wahren, Guten, Schönen,
Und hinter ihm, in wesenlosem Scheine,
Lag, was uns alle bändigt, das Gemeine.

Nun schmückt' er sich die schöne Gartenzinne,
Von wannen er der Sterne Wort vernahm,
Das dem gleich ew'gen, gleich lebend'gen Sinne

1. EPILOG TO SCHILLER'S "BELL."

> To the city joyful presage,
> Peace shall be its foremost message!

This came to pass! To greet the peaceful ringing
Our land was stirred to move; with blessings rare
A new-born happiness appeared: mid joyful singing
We welcomed back the young, the princely pair;
In thronging swarms, in crowds with new life winging,
The busy people mingled here and there,
And on the steps, festively decorated,
The "Homage of the Arts" was soon awaited.

I hear the midnight hush in terror rended,
A dull and heavy mourning bell has rung.
Is this for him, for him, our friend, intended,
To whom our every hope has firmly clung?
Shall his deserving life by death be ended?
In what dismay the world by this is flung!
Ah, what bereavement we, his friends, now reap!
The whole world weeps, and why should we not weep?

For he was ours! What charm and fascination
On happy days the noble man displayed.
How soon, from serious mood, with animation
To lighter conversation he was swayed;
Adroit and keen, with brilliant confirmation
He pondered deeper plans that life had laid,
In deed and counsel finding rich employment:
This has been our experience, our enjoyment.

For he was ours! May those words of pride
Drown out our clamorous cries of lamentation!
In our safe port, secure from storm and tide,
He well could seek his lasting habitation.
Meanwhile his titan soul did forward stride,
In Goodness, Truth, and Beauty found duration.
Behind him lay, to empty shadows faded,
The mean and base, which keeps us all degraded.

Now to his charming garden-wall he turned,
From where the message of the stars he heard,
Which found a soul that like them ever burned,

Geheimnisvoll und klar entgegenkam.
Dort, sich und uns zu köstlichem Gewinne,
Verwechselt' er die Zeiten wundersam,
Begegnet' so, im Würdigsten beschäftigt,
Der Dämmerung, der Nacht, die uns entkräftigt.

Ihm schwollen der Geschichte Flut auf Fluten,
Verspülend, was getadelt, was gelobt,
Der Erdbeherrscher wilde Heeresgluten,
Die in der Welt sich grimmig ausgetobt,
Im niedrig Schrecklichsten, im höchsten Guten
Nach ihrem Wesen deutlich durchgeprobt.—
Nun sank der Mond, und zu erneuter Wonne
Vom klaren Berg herüber stieg die Sonne.

Nun glühte seine Wange rot und röter
Von jener Jugend, die uns nie entfliegt,
Von jenem Mut, der, früher oder später,
Den Widerstand der stumpfen Welt besiegt,
Von jenem Glauben, der sich, stets erhöhter,
Bald kühn hervordrängt, bald geduldig schmiegt,
Damit das Gute wirke, wachse, fromme,
Damit der Tag dem Edlen endlich komme.

Doch hat er, so geübt, so vollgehaltig,
Dies bretterne Gerüste nicht verschmäht:
Hier schildert' er das Schicksal, das gewaltig
Von Tag zu Nacht die Erdenachse dreht,
Und manches tiefe Werk hat, reichgestaltig,
Den Wert der Kunst, des Künstlers Wert erhöht;
Er wendete die Blüte höchsten Strebens,
Das Leben selbst, an dieses Bild des Lebens.

Ihr kanntet ihn, wie er mit Riesenschritte
Den Kreis des Wollens, des Vollbringens mass,
Durch Zeit und Land, der Völker Sinn und Sitte,
Das dunkle Buch mit heitrem Blicke las;
Doch wie er, atemlos, in unsrer Mitte
In Leiden bangte, kümmerlich genas,
Das haben wir in traurig schönen Jahren,
Denn er war unser, leidend miterfahren.

Announcing clearly their mysterious way,
For self and us a rich reward he earned,
And wonderously transformed night into day,
And thus he met, in noblest occupation,
The dusk, the dark, that spells our enervation.

To him there came, in flood-tide, vanished ages
To wash away alike old praise and blame;
Each conquering army through the picture rages
That in the world had set its savage flame;
Their basely vile, their grandly noble stages—
He bares their nature and their every aim.
The moon now sank, and new delights to render,
From clear-cut hills the sun arose in splendor.

And soon his cheeks were flamed with crimson fire
Of endless youth, that no man's heart forsakes,
And of that strength that with a brave desire
The dull resistance of blunt spirits breaks,
And of that faith that, rising ever higher,
Now boldly, now with patience ever wakes,
That so the good shall work, increase, and flourish,
And noble men no idle hope shall nourish.

But he, so trained, and in his highest flower,
This boarded framework took to stage his plays:
Here limned a destiny whose mighty power
Our planet's axis spins through endless days,
And many a work profound, with richest dower,
The worth of art, the artist's worth did raise.
His highest gifts he used, in full devotion,
Yes, life itself, to paint our life's commotion.

You knew him, saw him like a giant measure
The range of will, fulfillment's certain tread;
Of times and lands, folklore and human treasure,
The obscure book with clear-eyed glance he read.
But when with us in forced and breathless leisure
He cringed with pain, and barely left his bed,
We suffered with him years of grief and gladness,
For he was ours, and with him bore his sadness.

Ihn, wenn er vom zerrüttenden Gewühle
Des bittren Schmerzes wieder aufgeblickt,
Ihn haben wir dem lästigen Gefühle
Der Gegenwart, der stockenden, entrückt,
Mit guter Kunst und ausgesuchtem Spiele
Den neubelebten edlen Sinn erquickt,
Und noch am Abend vor den letzten Sonnen
Ein holdes Lächeln glücklich abgewonnen.

Er hatte früh das strenge Wort gelesen,
Dem Leiden war er, war dem Tod vertraut.
So schied er nun, wie er so oft genesen;
Nun schreckt uns das, wofür uns längst gegraut.
Doch schon erblicket sein verklärtes Wesen
Sich hier verklärt, wenn es hernieder schaut:
Was Mitwelt sonst an ihm beklagt, getadelt,
Es hat's der Tod, es hat's die Zeit geadelt.

Auch manche Geister, die mit ihm gerungen,
Sein gross Verdienst unwillig anerkannt,
Sie fühlen sich von seiner Kraft durchdrungen,
In seinem Kreise willig festgebannt:
Zum Höchsten hat er sich emporgeschwungen,
Mit allem, was wir schätzen, eng verwandt.
So feiert ihn! Denn, was dem Mann das Leben
Nur halb erteilt, soll ganz die Nachwelt geben.

So bleibt er uns, der vor so manchen Jahren —
Schon zehne sind's!—von uns sich weggekehrt!
Wir haben alle segenreich erfahren,
Die Welt verdank' ihm, was er sie gelehrt:
Schon längst verbreitet sich's in ganze Scharen,
Das Eigenste, was ihm allein gehört.
Er glänzt uns vor, wie ein Komet entschwindend,
Unendlich Licht mit seinem Licht verbindend.

2. SCHILLERS RELIQUIEN

Im ernsten Beinhaus war's, wo ich beschaute,
Wie Schädel Schädeln angeordnet passten;
Die alte Zeit gedacht' ich, die ergraute.

When ended what had crushed him and dejected—
The bitter pain—, and he rejoined us here,
His thinking from the Present we deflected,
That seemed unmoving, burdensome, severe;
With kindly arts and pastimes well selected
His noble mind, refreshed, we sought to cheer;
And just before he went from us forever
A gracious smile rewarded our endeavor.

He early read his doom, the end decreeing;
He learned to suffer, heard the Reaper's tread.
At last he met the fate he had been fleeing;
We're shocked by that which long has been our dread.
But now he sees his own transfigured being
Transfigured here, as he stands overhead:
What once the world about him deprecated—
Death has ennobled, time eradicated.

And many men who oft with him contended,
And all his merits scarcely recognized,
Now feel his powers with their spirits blended,
And in his sphere are willingly comprised:
To highest heights his lofty mind ascended,
Yet closely kin to all we dearly prized.
So praise him! What in part the world had striven
To keep from him, must now in full be given.

So he remains, although ten years ago
He turned from us and our bereavement wrought;
We all have learned from him what debt we owe,
To our great blessing, for the things he taught:
They march forever, through the world they go.
His own distinctive views and work and thought.
He shines before us, cometlike declining,
Infinite light with his own light combining.

2. SCHILLER'S REMAINS

In that grim charnel house I was, surveying
How dense the rows of skulls on shelves were mated;
Of olden times I thought and their decaying.

Sie stehn in Reih' geklemmt, die sonst sich hassten,
   Und derbe Knochen, die sich tödlich schlugen,
   Sie liegen kreuzweis, zahm allhier zu rasten.

Entrenkte Schulterblätter! was sie trugen,
   Fragt niemand mehr, und zierlich tät'ge Glieder,
   Die Hand, der Fuss, zerstreut aus Lebensfugen.

Ihr Müden also lagt vergebens nieder,
   Nicht Ruh im Grabe liess man euch, vertrieben
   Seid ihr herauf zum lichten Tage wieder,

Und niemand kann die dürre Schale lieben,
   Welch herrlich edlen Kern sie auch bewahrte.
   Doch mir Adepten war die Schrift geschrieben,

Die heil'gen Sinn nicht jedem offenbarte,
   Als ich inmitten solcher starren Menge
   Unschätzbar herrlich ein Gebild gewahrte,

Dass in des Raumes Moderkält' und Enge
   Ich frei und wärmefühlend mich erquickte,
   Als ob ein Lebensquell dem Tod entspränge.

Wie mich geheimnisvoll die Form entzückte!
   Die gottgedachte Spur, die sich erhalten!
   Ein Blick, der mich an jenes Meer entrückte,

Das flutend strömt gesteigerte Gestalten.
   Geheim Gefäss, Orakelsprüche spendend!
   Wie bin ich wert, dich in der Hand zu halten,

Dich höchsten Schatz aus Moder fromm entwendend
   Und in die freie Luft, zu freiem Sinnen,
   Zum Sonnenlicht andächtig hin mich wendend?

Was kann der Mensch im Leben mehr gewinnen,
   Als dass sich Gott-Natur ihm offenbare:
   Wie sie das Feste lässt zu Geist verrinnen,
   Wie sie das Geisterzeugte fest bewahre.

3.   GEDICHTE SIND GEMALTE FENSTERSCHEIBEN

Gedichte sind gemalte Fensterscheiben!
Sieht man vom Markt in die Kirche hinein,

In close-packed rows they stand, though deep they hated,
And hardy bones, in mortal strife once faring,
Are lying crosswise, tame, their strife abated.

Disjointed shoulder blades! What they have faced
No man now asks; these dainty limbs must sever,
These hands and feet, from frames that once they graced.

Weary you are, in vain from your endeavor
You sought to rest; from peaceful graves you're driven
Again to daylight that you left forever.

No one can love the husk, thus dried and riven,
However fine a kernel once concealing.
To me, adept, however, there was given

A scroll, its high sense not to all revealing,
When I, in passing many a rigid figure,
Discerned a shape unspeakably appealing,

So that amid this chilling mould and rigor
I felt refreshed with free and warm emotion,
As though from death life's fount shot forth in vigor.

This form aroused such mystic rapt devotion!
God-given lineaments that naught erases!
A glance that took me to the distant ocean,

Whose flood-tide rolls up mightier forms and faces,
Mysterious vessel, oracles unfolding!
Would I be fit to hold you in embraces,

Dear treasure, freeing you from musty prison,
While I seek open sky and time for musing,
With reverence for the sunlight newly risen?

What more can life give mortals for their using
Than that God-Nature grant this revelation:
How it sends matter into spirit fusing,
How spirit-born achieves substantiation.

3. A POEM IS A STAINED-GLASS WINDOW PANE

A poem is a stained-glass window pane!
Look into the church from the market-place,

Da ist alles dunkel und düster;
Und so sieht's auch der Herr Philister.
Der mag denn wohl verdriesslich sein
Und lebenslang verdriesslich bleiben.

Kommt aber nur einmal herein,
Begrüsst die heilige Kapelle!
Da ist's auf einmal farbig helle:
Geschicht' und Zierat glänzt in Schnelle,
Bedeutend wirkt ein edler Schein.
Dies wird euch Kindern Gottes taugen,
Erbaut euch und ergetzt die Augen!

4. EIN GLEICHNIS

Jüngst pflückt' ich einen Wiesenstrauss,
Trug ihn gedankenvoll nach Haus,
Da hatten von der warmen Hand
Die Kronen sich alle zur Erde gewandt.
Ich setzte sie in frisches Glas,
Und welch ein Wunder war mir das!
Die Köpfchen hoben sich empor,
Die Blätterstengel im grünen Flor,
Und allzusammen so gesund,
Als stünden sie noch auf Muttergrund.

So war mir's, als ich wundersam
Mein Lied in fremder Sprache vernahm.

5. GEFUNDEN

Ich ging im Walde
So für mich hin,
Und nichts zu suchen,
Das war mein Sinn.

Im Schatten sah ich
Ein Blümchen stehn,
Wie Sterne leuchtend,
Wie Äuglein schön.

Ich wollt' es brechen,
Da sagt' es fein:

Note how dark all seems to the view;
So Mr. Humdrum sees it too.
Vexed, he'll show a petulant face
And all his life will so remain.

But now step in for a closer view
And greet the chapel consecrated!
There's sheen and color variegated
And story and art illuminated,
While noble light has meaning true.
God's children, things like this you'll prize,
Be edified and feast your eyes!

4. PARABLE

I picked wild flowers recently
And took a bunch home thoughtfully;
The warmth that by my hand was shed
Made every flower droop its head.
I gave them water in a glass,
And what a miracle came to pass!
The little heads perked up once more,
The stems were greening as before,
And all in all they looked so well
As when they grew in their native dell.

I felt that way when I heard my song
Wondrously in a foreign tongue.

5. FOUND

Just strolling along
In the woods I went,
And on no purpose
Was I intent.

I saw in the shade
A flower there,
Like starlight beaming,
Like eyes so fair.

I wished to pick it,
When gently it said:

Soll ich zum Welken
Gebrochen sein?

Ich grub's mit allen
Den Würzlein aus,
Zum Garten trug ich's
Am hübschen Haus.

Und pflanzt' es wieder
Am stillen Ort;
Nun zweigt es immer
Und blüht so fort.

6. DEM AUFGEHENDEN VOLLMONDE

Dornburg, 25. August 1828

Willst du mich sogleich verlassen?
Warst im Augenblick so nah!
Dich umfinstern Wolkenmassen,
Und nun bist du gar nicht da.

Doch du fühlst, wie ich betrübt bin,
Blickt dein Rand herauf als Stern!
Zeugest mir, dass ich geliebt bin,
Sei das Liebchen noch so fern.

So hinan denn! hell und heller,
Reiner Bahn, in voller Pracht!
Schlägt mein Herz auch schmerzlich schneller,
Überselig ist die Nacht.

7. DORNBURG, SEPTEMBER 1828

Früh, wenn Tal, Gebirg und Garten
Nebelschleiern sich enthüllen
Und dem sehnlichsten Erwarten
Blumenkelche bunt sich füllen;

Wenn der Äther, Wolken tragend,
Mit dem klaren Tage streitet
Und ein Ostwind, sie verjagend,
Blaue Sonnenbahn bereitet;

"Shall I be broken
To wilt and lie dead?"

With its roots and all
I dug it free,
To the lovely house
I took it with me.

In the garden I found it
A quiet place;
Now ever it thrives
And blooms apace.

6. TO THE RISING FULL MOON

Dornburg, August 25, 1828

Ah, so soon you'd leave me pining?
Winks ago you seemed so near!
Banks of clouds conceal your shining,
Now you are no longer here.

But you feel how I am saddened
When your brim is like a star,
Proving that I should be gladdened
By a love, however far.

Rise with bright and brighter glamour
On your course in splendor dight!
Harder though my sick heart hammer,
Yet, how blissful is the night.

7. DORNBURG, SEPTEMBER, 1828

When, at dawn, dale, hills, and bower
Shed the mist that on them lies,
And the chalice of the flower
Fills to charm our longing eyes;

When in ether, clouds are carried
And with sunshine would contend,
When an east wind clouds has harried,
Sky-blue sunlight to extend;

Dankst du dann, am Blick dich weidend,
Reiner Brust der Grossen, Holden,
Wird die Sonne, rötlich scheidend,
Rings den Horizont vergolden.

8.- 17. SPRÜCHE

8.   Wo Anmassung mir wohlgefällt?
An Kindern; denen gehört die Welt.

      *   *   *

9.   Wenn ein Edler gegen dich fehlt,
So tu, als hättest du's nicht gezählt;
Er wird es in sein Schuldbuch schreiben
Und dir nicht lange im Debet bleiben.

      *   *   *

10.   Ein reiner Reim wird wohl begehrt;
Doch den Gedanken rein zu haben,
Die edelste von allen Gaben,
Das ist mir alle Reime wert.

      *   *   *

11.   Vom Vater hab' ich die Statur,
Des Lebens ernstes Führen,
Vom Mütterchen die Frohnatur
Und Lust zu fabulieren.
Urahnherr war der Schönsten hold,
Das spukt so hin und wieder;
Urahnfrau liebte Schmuck und Gold,
Das zuckt wohl durch die Glieder.

      *   *   *

12.   DEN VEREINIGTEN STAATEN

Amerika, du hast es besser
Als unser Kontinent, das alte,
Hast keine verfallene Schlösser
Und keine Basalte.
Dich stört nicht im Innern,
Zu lebendiger Zeit,
Unnützes Erinnern
Und vergeblicher Streit.

      *   *   *

Give the sun pure thanks, admire
All his great and kindly powers:
Then with crimson flush he'll fire
Gold horizons as he lowers.

8.- 17. EPIGRAMS AND SAYINGS

8.   Where does presumptuousness have merit?
In children. The world is theirs to inherit.

* * *

9.   When noble men have done you ill,
Then act as though it counted nil.
They'll book it as their debit yet
And soon will pay you back the debt.

* * *

10.   A rhyme that's pure is sought and hoped for,
But keeping thought unspoiled and pure:—
The noblest gift of which we're sure—
Is worth all rhymes I've ever groped for.

* * *

11.   I have my stature from papa,
My way of life so stable;
My cheerful bent from dear mama,
And delight in tale and fable.
With fair maids ancestors made bold,
I still can sense that itching;
Ancestress loved fine stones and gold,
My limbs too feel such twitching.

* * *

12. TO THE UNITED STATES

America, you're better off
Than our own continent that's old.
At tumble-down castles you scoff,
You lack basalt, I'm told.
Within, nothing daunts you
In times rife with life,
No memory haunts you
Nor vain, idle strife.

* * *

13. GESELLSCHAFT

Aus einer grossen Gesellschaft heraus
Ging einst ein stiller Gelehrter zu Haus.
Man fragte: Wie seid ihr zufrieden gewesen?
„Wären's Bücher," sagt er, „ich würd' sie nicht lesen."

    *   *   *

14. BREIT WIE LANG

Wer bescheiden ist, muss dulden,
Und wer frech ist, der muss leiden;
Also wirst du gleich verschulden,
Ob du froh bist, ob bescheiden.

    *   *   *

15. LEBENSREGEL

Willst du dir ein hübsch Leben zimmern,
Musst dich ums Vergangene nicht bekümmern;
Das wenigste muss dich verdriessen;
Musst stets die Gegenwart geniessen,
Besonders keinen Menschen hassen
Und die Zukunft Gott überlassen.

    *   *   *

16. FRISCHES EI, GUTES EI

Enthusiasmus vergleich' ich gern
Der Auster, meine lieben Herrn,
Die, wenn Ihr sie nicht frisch genosst,
Wahrhaftig ist eine schlechte Kost,
Begeistrung ist keine Heringsware,
Die man einpökelt auf einige Jahre.

    *   *   *

17. Wie das Gestirn,
Ohne Hast,
Aber ohne Rast,
Drehe sich jeder
Um die eigne Last.

18. PROŒMION

I.

Im Namen dessen, der sich selbst erschuf,
Von Ewigkeit in schaffendem Beruf;

13. GUESTS AT A PARTY

From a party to which many guests had come
A quiet scholar had just gone home.
A friend asked: Were you satisfied?
"Were they books, I would not have read them," he cried.

*   *   *

14. AS BROAD AS IT IS LONG

If you're meek, you must endure,
If you're pert, then grief's your lot;
Thus of trouble you are sure,
Meek or pert, it matters not.

*   *   *

15. RULE FOR LIVING

In case a good life you would earn,
For bygones show no great concern.
By very few things be annoyed;
The present time must be enjoyed,
But hate no man in any case,
And leave the future to Heaven's grace.

*   *   *

16. FRESH EGG, GOOD EGG

Enthusiasm, I would say,
Is like an oyster in many a way,
Which, if not fresh the time you eat,
Is deemed no enviable treat.
A pickled herring will last and last,
Enthusiasm spoils too fast.

*   *   *

17.   Like stars above,
        Without haste,
        But steadfastly paced,
        Revolve round the duties
        With which you are faced.

18. PROŒMION

I.

In His blest name, Himself His own creation,
Forevermore creative in vocation;

In seinem Namen, der den Glauben schafft,
Vertrauen, Liebe, Tätigkeit und Kraft;
In jenes Namen, der, so oft genannt,
Dem Wesen nach blieb immer unbekannt.

So weit das Ohr, so weit das Auge reicht,
Du findest nur Bekanntes, das ihm gleicht,
Und deines Geistes höchster Feuerflug
Hat schon am Gleichnis, hat am Bild genug;
Es zieht dich an, es reisst dich heiter fort,
Und wo du wandelst, schmückt sich Weg und Ort.
Du zählst nicht mehr, berechnest keine Zeit,
Und jeder Schritt ist Unermesslichkeit.

II.
Was wär' ein Gott, der nur von aussen stiesse,
Im Kreis das All am Finger laufen liesse!
Ihm ziemt's, die Welt im Innern zu bewegen,
Natur in sich, sich in Natur zu hegen,
So dass, was in ihm lebt und webt und ist,
Nie seine Kraft, nie seinen Geist vermisst.

III.
Im Innern ist ein Universum auch;
Daher der Völker löblicher Gebrauch,
Dass jeglicher das Beste, was er kennt,
Er Gott, ja seinen Gott benennt,
Ihm Himmel und Erden übergibt,
Ihn fürchtet, und wo möglich liebt.

19. EINS UND ALLES

Im Grenzenlosen sich zu finden,
Wird gern der einzelne verschwinden,
Da löst sich aller Überdruss;
Statt heissem Wünschen, wildem Wollen,
Statt läst'gem Fordern, strengem Sollen
Sich aufzugeben ist Genuss.

Weltseele, komm, uns zu durchdringen!
Dann mit dem Weltgeist selbst zu ringen,
Wird unsrer Kräfte Hochberuf.

In His blest name who makes all faith to be,
All trust and love, all strength and energy;
In His blest name whom men do oft profess,
But whose true essence we can never guess.

So far as ear can hear or eye's not dim,
All known things, you will find, are like to Him.
The highest flight that mind of man e'er bore
Resorts to simile or metaphor;
Attracting you, it carries you away,
And where you go, both path and place are gay.
No more you count, nor calculate the time,
And every step's infinity sublime.

II.

What god at work in outer space would linger
And let the universe spin round his finger!
Fitter it is, He'd give things inward motion,
Fill Self and World with mutual devotion,
That all which in Him lives and weaves and grows
His power and His spirit shares and knows.

III.

Within us too a universe doth dwell;
Wherefore I like the people's habit well,
That each man on the Best Thing that he knows,
The name of God—his God—bestows;
Man grants Him earth and heaven above
And shows Him fear and sometimes love.

19. ONE AND ALL

To find their place where bounds are banished
Lone mortal men have gladly vanished,
And gone is everything that cloys;
Instead of wishes, rash demanding,
Annoying plea, and stern commanding,
Renounce your will, and yours are joys.

World-Soul, o make your impulse ours!
Then wrestling with World-Spirit's powers
Will be our highest duty's call.

Teilnehmend führen gute Geister,
Gelinde leitend, höchste Meister,
Zu dem, der alles schafft und schuf.

Und umzuschaffen das Geschaffne,
Damit sich's nicht zum Starren waffne,
Wirkt ewiges, lebend'ges Tun.
Und was nicht war, nun will es werden
Zu reinen Sonnen, farb'gen Erden;
In keinem Falle darf es ruhn.

Es soll sich regen, schaffend handeln,
Erst sich gestalten, dann verwandeln;
Nur scheinbar steht's Momente still.
Das Ew'ge regt sich fort in allen;
Denn alles muss in Nichts zerfallen,
Wenn es im Sein beharren will.

20. DAUER IM WECHSEL

Hielte diesen frühen Segen,
Ach, nur eine Stunde fest!
Aber vollen Blütenregen
Schüttelt schon der laue West.
Soll ich mich des Grünen freuen,
Dem ich Schatten erst verdankt?
Bald wird Sturm auch das zerstreuen,
Wenn es falb im Herbst geschwankt.

Willst du nach den Früchten greifen,
Eilig nimm dein Teil davon!
Diese fangen an, zu reifen,
Und die andern keimen schon;
Gleich mit jedem Regengusse,
Ändert sich dein holdes Tal,
Ach, und in demselben Flusse
Schwimmst du nicht zum zweitenmal.

Du nun selbst! Was felsenfeste
Sich vor dir hervorgetan,
Mauern siehst du, siehst Paläste
Stets mit andern Augen an.

Kind spirits, showing helpful features,
Will lead us well, as highest teachers,
To Him that made and fashions all.

To recreate what was created,
That by no rigor it be weighted,
Unending, living deeds are best.
And what was not, will now take life:
Pure suns and world with colors rife;
And by no means shall there be rest.

't must stir and change in new creation,
First take on form, then transformation;
Not long does it appear to rest.
The eternal stirs and works for ay;
For everything must once decay
If it would live to stand the test.

20. STABILITY IN CHANGE

Ah, could but a single hour
Hold these boons with which we're blest!
Soon though comes a blossom-shower
Swept by soft winds from the West.
Shall such verdure cause me joy?
Lately still it gave me shade.
Soon too tempests will destroy
Leaves that sway in fall and fade.

Do the fruits not seem alluring?
Take a share, for you to cull!
Some already are maturing,
While the others blossom full;
Every rain that comes to pound
Will transform your dale sublime,
Ah, but in those floods that bound
You'll not swim a second time.

You yourself! What fixed and steady
Seemed unalterable to you—
Walls and palaces already
Change before your very view.

Weggeschwunden ist die Lippe,
Die im Kusse sonst genas,
Jener Fuss, der an der Klippe
Sich mit Gemsenfreche mass.

Jene Hand, die gern und milde
Sich bewegte, wohlzutun,
Das gegliederte Gebilde,
Alles ist ein andres nun.
Und was sich an Jener Stelle
Nun mit deinem Namen nennt,
Kam herbei wie eine Welle,
Und so eilt's zum Element.

Lass den Anfang mit dem Ende
Sich in Eins zusammenziehn!
Schneller als die Gegenstände
Selber dich vorüberfliehn!
Danke, dass die Gunst der Musen
Unvergängliches verheisst:
Den Gehalt in deinem Busen
Und die Form in deinem Geist.

21. VORSPRUCH

Weite Welt und breites Leben,
Lange Jahre, redlich Streben,
Stets geforscht und stets gegründet,
Nie geschlossen, oft geründet,
Ältestes bewahrt mit Treue,
Freundlich aufgefasstes Neue,
Heitern Sinn und reine Zwecke:
Nun, man kommt wohl eine Strecke.

22. LIED DES TÜRMERS

Zum Sehen geboren,
Zum Schauen bestellt,
Dem Turme geschworen,
Gefällt mir die Welt.

Gone the lips and all their blisses
That in kissing once were tense,
Gone the foot at precipices
With a chamois' insolence.

And that hand, so freely giving,
Stirring for the good and right,
Every organism living—
All have changed before our sight.
And whoso That Place is taking
That with your name once was blent,
Came like some huge billow breaking,
Hastening toward its element.

Let Beginning now and Ending
Merge and fuse into a One!
Swifter than all things attending,
Let your flight be sooner done!
Thankful that the Muses' favor
Brings a boon that ever lives:
Substance born of heart's endeavor
And the form your spirit gives.

21. MOTTO

Spacious world, capacious life,
Years with honest effort rife,
Tireless searching, firmly founded,
Never ended, often rounded,
Old traditions well respected,
Innovations not rejected,
Noble aim, with cheer professed:
Well, we're sure that we've progressed.

22. SONG OF THE TOWER KEEPER

For seeing I'm born
And appointed for sight,
To the tower I'm sworn,
And the world's my delight.

Ich blick' in die Ferne,
Ich seh' in der Näh'
Den Mond und die Sterne,
Den Wald und das Reh.

So seh' ich in allen
Die ewige Zier,
Und wie mir's gefallen,
Gefall' ich auch mir.

Ihr glücklichen Augen,
Was je ihr gesehn,
Es sei wie es wolle,
Es war doch so schön!

I gaze on the Far,
And I look at the Near;
The moon and each star,
And the forest and deer.

A beauty eternal
In all these I see,
And as it has pleased me,
I'm pleasing to me.

You eyes, o how happy,
Of all you have seen,
Whatever it might be,
How fair it has been!

Appendix

Musical Settings to the Poems

A statistical article published in 1912 in the trade journal of the German book dealers (*Börsenblatt für den deutschen Buchhandel*) by Ernst Challier, makes it clear that only three German lyrists have found more composers than Goethe. Heine rates highest by far, and he is followed by Geibel and Hoffmann von Fallersleben, the author of the German national anthem. At the time he wrote in 1912, Challier had counted 2660 musical compositions for works of Goethe. Since then this number has risen.

As these statistics suggest, the number of compositions that a poet's lyrics have evoked is by no means an unfailing criterion for his rank as a poet. If it were otherwise, then second or third-rate poets like Geibel, Hoffmann von Fallersleben, Reinick, and Baumbach, all of whom are among the first ten on the list, could be classed with Goethe, Eichendorff, and Mörike as poets of the highest water. Evanescent popularity, sentimentality, simplicity of thought-content, and even shallowness and superficial musical quality are the very factors that attract many composers, though usually not the best. In Goethe's case, the music inherent in his poems sometimes makes musical composition well-nigh unnecessary.

The history of the German *lied* begins with Gluck (1714-1787) in the middle of the eighteenth century and is carried forward by Mozart (1756-1791), Beethoven (1770-1827), and lesser lights like J. F. Reichardt (1752-1814) and K. F. Zelter (1758-1832). With Franz Schubert (1798-1828) the *lied* reaches a high plane of excellence during the latter years of Goethe's life. Schubert, besides being the first of the truly great composers of *lieder*, was also the first to break away from the artificiality of the stanzaic structure of the *lied* and to suit his music to the varying moods of each succeeding stanza, casting not the stanza, but the poem as a whole in a unified and suitable melodic mould. This is expressed by the term *durchkomponieren*.

Almost on a par with Schubert is Robert Schumann (1810-1856), only twelve years his junior. Carl Loewe (1796-1869), famous for his ballads, was their contemporary, though not their equal. Felix Mendelssohn-Bartholdy (1809-1847) and

Robert Franz (1815-1892) worked in the spirit of the masters, but lacked their depth as well as their ability. More can be said for Johannes Brahms (1833-1897), who also derived his inspiration from Schubert. He roamed almost the entire field of German lyric poetry for inspiration and richly found it, but often let his music overshadow the poet's text.

Greater than all these in the field of the *lied,* except Schubert himself, is Hugo Wolf (1860-1903). No composer has taken such pains to immerse himself in the poets and the poems of his choice as did Wolf. He always regarded himself first and foremost as the faithful interpreter of the poet's spirit and meaning. Consequently he "specialized" in individual poets for longer periods of time. Beginning in October, 1888, for instance, he devoted an entire year to setting 53 Goethe poems to music.

Among more recent composers who have devoted their talents to the German lyrists of the eighteenth, as well as the nineteenth and twentieth centuries, the most gifted was Richard Strauss. Of Americans we find Ethelbert Nevin and Frank van der Stucken.

In preparing the following necessarily brief and incomplete summary of musical settings to the poems appearing in this volume, the work of Max Friedländer, *Das deutsche Lied im 18. Jahrhundert* (2 volumes, 1902), as well as the many scores published by the same authority in volumes 11 (1891) and 31 (1916) of the *Schriften der Goethe-Gesellschaft* (hereafter abbreviated as SGG), have been helpful. Some of these scores are referred to below. For supplementary statistics Challier's *Grosser Liederkatalog* (15. Nachtrag, Giessen, 1914) is of some value, as is also Ewald A. Boucke's *Goethes Gedichte*, Ausgewählt, eingeleitet, und erläutert, Leipzig n.d. [1927], Appendix.

For further brief but specific information on Goethe's poems set to music, see the three-page note (written by Friedländer) in *The Life of Goethe* by Albert Bielschowsky, translated by William A. Cooper (III, 374 ff.).

Chapter **I, 1, 2**: both composed by Bernhard Theodor Breitkopf in 1769, without credit being given to Goethe.

II, 1: at least 45 compositions, the first by Reichardt (1781), the best by Beethoven (op. 52, no. 4; SGG 1916).

2: over 100, the earliest by von Dalberg (1793), the best by Schubert (op. 3, no. 3; SGG 1896); also one by Schumann (op.

67, no. 3) and one in Brahms' *Volks-Kinderlieder* (based on Schubert). The best-known popular setting, by Heinrich Werner, is under Schubert's influence. There are settings for solo, duets, mixed, and male choruses. Schubert was greatly inspired by Goethe's poems. On the day he, then eighteen, composed the "Rose in the Heather" he also set eight other Goethe poems to music.

3: at least 20, the best by Beethoven (op. 83, no. 3; SGG 1896).

4: by Petersen Grönland, 1817, and W. Weissheimer, about 1896.

5: Schubert's (op. 56, no. 1) surpasses earlier ones of Reichardt and Grönland.

Goethe wrote some of the Friederike songs to melodies then popular, which she sang. Some new settings in Lehar's *Friederike*.

III, 1: a fine composition by Schubert (op. 19, no. 1), together with others sent with a modest letter to Goethe, was not even acknowledged.

2: another fine composition by Schubert (SGG 1916), far surpassing Reichardt's and even Wolf's no. 49 of the Goethe cycle.

3: again Schubert (op. 19, no. 3) surpasses others, at least four in number, including Wolf.

4: earliest composition, known also to Goethe, by P. C. Kayser (1775); at least four others, including two by Reichardt (1798).

5: over 25, by Reichardt (twice), Beethoven (op. 75, no. 2; SGG 1916: the best), Zelter, etc.

6: over 15, the best by Mendelssohn-Bartholdy for mixed quartet (op. 41, no. 6) and by Schubert (op. 92, no. 2).

7: by Reichardt, 1794, and C. Erfurt.

8: by Reichardt, 1809, and C. Bering, 1906.

10: by B. Scholz, op. 44, no. 4.

11: well composed by Reichardt (in Friedländer's *Das deutsche Lied im 18. Jahrhundert*, exhibit 134), Schubert (op. 3, no. 4), and Zelter; less successfully by about forty others.

IV, 1: at least 70, Schubert's being by far the best (op. 5, no. 1; SGG 1916). Immediately after reading this poem, Schubert was ecstatically moved to set it to music. Two composi-

tions by Reichardt are also good. Beethoven has left a draft
of a composition.

3: by Schubert and E. Mattiesen, op. 5, no. 1 (1921).

4: seven, two by Schubert for male octette (*Gesamtausgabe*,
1891; op. 167). Loewe's is the next best.

5: among four compositions, Schubert's (SGG 1896) sur-
passes that of Wolf.

6: by Beethoven (canon for eight voices) and several others.

8: about 50, two by Schubert, but little known (the first
in fascicle 47, no. 5, posthumous; the second in SGG 1896, but
also in *Nachgelassene 6 Lieder*, no. 3, Berlin, 1868). His second
is superior. Pfitzner, op. 18.

10: of the thirty compositions, Beethoven's (op. 83, no. 1;
SGG 1896) is best, surpassing Schubert's early effort. F. van
der Stucken, op. 5, no. 5.

11: already printed with music by P. C. Kayser in 1780 in
a Zurich magazine; it pleased Goethe. In all, the poem has been
composed over 150 times (by Reichardt twice, by Zelter, Schu-
bert, Weber, Loewe, and Liszt), but no setting is quite satis-
factory.

12: over 200, among them one by Liszt; the best, Schubert's
(op. 96, no. 3; SGG 1916). Friedrich Kuhlau's setting for male
choir is also popular. Some of the compositions are set to a
trivialized text. Goethe liked Zelter's anemic effort (SGG
1896). Anton Rubinstein's setting, a duet (op. 48, no. 5) uses
a Russian translation by Lermontoff. For a setting by Liszt,
see SGG 1916.

13: over 50, the best by Schubert (op. 5, no. 4) and H. G.
Nägeli (SGG 1896). Reichardt, Zelter (SGG 1916), and Men-
delssohn-Bartholdy were less successful with it. Wolf, 1876.

V, 1: about 100, several by non-Germans (Rubinstein, Tchai-
kovsky, Ambroise Thomas), also Reichardt, Zelter (two), Beet-
hoven (op. 75, no. 1), Schubert and Liszt. We are told that
Goethe was moved by Beethoven's setting, but he preferred not
only that of the Czech Tomaschek, but also Reichardt's effort.
Today Beethoven's is deemed best, but one by F. H. Himmel
is more popular. See Erck's *Liederschatz* I. Schubert's (fasc.
20, posthumous), Schumann's two (op. 79, no. 29, and op. 98,
no. 1) and Liszt's (*Gesammelte Lieder*, no. 1) are less satis-
factory. There are also several parodies set to music. For
Reichardt, Tomaschek, Beethoven, and Spontini see SGG 1896.

2: at least 70. Reichardt and Zelter wrote two settings each, Beethoven four (SGG 1916), and Schubert six (four solos, the best known op. 62, no. 4, one duet, and one quintet; see SGG 1896). Schumann's setting is op. 98, no. 3. Tchaikovsky's (op. 6, no. 6) is widely known. One of Zelter's settings is reproduced in SGG 1916.

3: over 20 by Reichardt, Zelter (SGG 1896), Schubert two (in *Gesamtausgabe*, 1895; op. 12, no. 1; SGG 1916), Schumann (op. 96, no. 6), Rubinstein (op. 91, no. 3), etc.

4: over 35 by Reichardt, Zelter two, Schubert three (op. 12, no. 2; the other two in *Gesamtausgabe*, 1895), Schumann (op. 98, no. 4), Rubinstein (op. 91, no. 2), Liszt two (*Gesammelte Lieder*, no. 5 and 41), etc. Schubert's op. 12, no. 2 is by far the best.

VI, 2: by Panofka, op. 64.

3: at least 35, among them the original one of Johann André (1775), one by Duchess Anna Amalia of Weimar, two by Reichardt, one by J. A. Steffan, and (the best) a dramatic scene by Mozart. All are in SGG 1896.

4: about 30, the best by Beethoven (op. 84, no. 4); Reichardt's is also good. Zelter, Schubert, Liszt (SGG 1916) and Rubinstein (op. 57) have set the song to music also. Since 1822 four additional (spurious) verses have often been sung.

5: at least 80 are known. Zelter's (SGG 1896) surpasses all others he has done; it remains popular. Still better ones are by Schubert (op. 5, no. 5), Berlioz (*Huit Scènes de Faust*, 1828; also SGG 1896), and Gounod (in his opera).

6: at least 35 exist, e.g. by L. Spohr (op. 52, no. 2); Zelter; seventeen-year-old Schubert (op. 2; SGG 1916), which is the best; Berlioz; Richard Wagner (op. 5), etc. Beethoven has left only a draft (about 1810).

7: over 20: Reichardt, Zelter, C. Schreiber—popular for a long time—, Schubert op. 117, Schumann op. 91, no. 1 (SGG 1916), and Rubinstein op. 91, no. 1. But none stands out.

8: over 70. Reichardt's and Zelter's are satisfactory, but Schubert's, (op. 5), written at seventeen, is again the best. Zelter's and Schubert's are in SGG 1896.

9: about 50, including a duet and a chorus for male voices. The earliest, composed and sung by the actress Corona Schröter at the première of the melodrama *Die Fischerin* in 1782, proved very effective, as it did on another occasion over a hundred years later, because of its simplicity. Reichardt's is very good, Schubert's (op. 1) fine, but too sentimentally sensuous. It was the first Goethe song he composed. Beethoven left a draft. But the best of all is probably Loewe's (op. 1, no. 3). Noteworthy too is a setting by the nineteenth-century novelist Otto Ludwig. For the compositions of Schröter, Reichardt, Bernhard Klein, Zelter, Schubert, and Loewe, see SGG 1896.

10: at least six, Loewe's (op. 20, no. 2) and the symphonic poem by Paul Dukas being the best.

12: at least five: Zelter (SGG 1916), Schubert, Loewe, Klein, etc. Klein's is probably the best of these. In addition there are a three-act opera Les Bayadères by Catel (1810) and a more popular two-act opera by Auber (1830), with a text by Scribe.

13: a popular well-known melody is by Zelter; another by Eberwein (SGG 1916) has become known as a student song.

14: by Reichardt 1809, Tomaschek, op. 61, no. 2, and three or four others.

15: about 100, the best by Schubert (op. 5, no. 2; SGG 1896) and Beethoven (SGG 1916). Zelter's (SGG 1916) would probably rate third. For one by Himmel see SGG 1916.

16: about thirty, the best by Schubert (op. 3, no. 4), Beethoven (quartet, op. 112), Reichardt, Tomaschek (op. 60, no. 3). This poem and the next (17) inspired Mendelssohn-Bartholdy's Third Concert Ouverture (op. 28). Rubinstein and Goldmark provided male choruses.

17: same as 16.

18: set to music by Reichardt (see score in SGG 1916). The poem was written to an older melody then popular.

19: about 30, the first a song in the opera of Cimarosa, for a German version of which Goethe wrote his poem. The best is Tomaschek's (op. 54, no. 2). For both see SGG 1896. Also by Wolf, 1889, Ethelbert Nevin (op. 3, no. 2) and F. van der Stucken, 1903.

20: about 50. For the setting of Robert Franz (op. 33, no. 3) see SGG 1916.

VII, 6: Reichardt, 1789; Zelter, 1811; Wolf, 1888, and others.

VIII: The best settings of songs from the *West-Easterly Divan* are to be found in "*Suleika und Geheimes aus dem West-Östlichen Divan von Goethe,* in Musik gesetzt von Franz Schubert,*" 14. Werk, Vienna, 1822. 3 by Loewe, op. 22, no. 5; Liszt;

and Schumann, op. 25, no. 2 and op. 141; about five others. 6 by Zelter and Mendelssohn-Bartholdy. 10 by R. Kahn, op. 55, no. 6, and H. Huber, op. 69 (chorus). 11 by Eberwein, 1820, and Zelter 1823.

IX, 5: over 80, among them settings by Klein, Zelter, and Richard Strauss, op. 56, no. 1 (SGG 1916).

6: at least four little known compositions exist: e.g. E. E. Taubert, op. 71, no. 3, (about 1913).

7: by T. Streicher, op. 6, no. 3 (1897) and A. Urspruch, op. 30, no. 6.

18: by W. Kienzel, op. 103, no. 4 (about 1921).

20: by Reichardt, 1809, and Grönland, 1817.

22: See J. Simon, *Faust in der Musik*, Berlin, 1906. This song is included in the incidental *Faust* music of the British composer Henry Hugh Pierson (1816-1873), who spent much of his life in Germany.

In conclusion, the curious fact may be noted that one of the renowned composers of Goethe's time, P. E. Bach, ignored his poems.

The English renderings of this volume have been tried out with many of the available musical settings mentioned above.

INDEX

UNIVERSITY OF NORTH CAROLINA
STUDIES IN THE GERMANIC LANGUAGES
AND LITERATURES

1. Herbert W. Reichert. THE BASIC CONCEPTS IN THE PHILOSOPHY OF GOTTFRIED KELLER 1949. Pp. 164. Paper $ 3.00.
2. Olga Marx and Ernst Morwitz. THE WORKS OF STEFAN GEORGE. Rendered into English. 1949. Out of print.
3. Paul H. Curts. HEROD AND MARIAMNE, A Tragedy in Five Acts by Friedrich Hebbel, Translated into English Verse. 1950. Out of print.
4. Frederic E. Coenen. FRANZ GRILLPARZER'S PORTRAITURE OF MEN. 1951. Pp. xii, 135. Cloth $ 3.50.
5. Edwin H. Zeydel and B. Q. Morgan. THE PARZIVAL OF WOLFRAM VON ESCHENBACH. Translated into English Verse, with Introductions, Notes, and Connecting Summaries. 1951, 1956, 1960. Pp. xii, 370. Paper $ 4.50.
6. James C. O'Flaherty. UNITY AND LANGUAGE: A STUDY IN THE PHILOSOPHY OF JOHANN GEORG HAMANN. 1952. Out of print.
7. Sten G. Flygt. FRIEDRICH HEBBEL'S CONCEPTION OF MOVEMENT IN THE ABSOLUTE AND IN HISTORY. 1952. Out of print.
8. Richard Kuehnemund. ARMINIUS OR THE RISE OF A NATIONAL SYMBOL. (From Hutten to Grabbe.) 1953. Pp. xxx, 122. Cloth $ 3.50.
9. Lawrence S. Thompson. WILHELM WAIBLINGER IN ITALY. 1953. Pp. ix, 105. Paper $ 3.00.
10. Frederick Hiebel. NOVALIS. GERMAN POET - EUROPEAN THINKER - CHRISTIAN MYSTIC. 1953. Pp. xii, 126. 2nd rev. ed. 1959. Paper $ 3.50.
11. Walter Silz. Realism and Reality: Studies in the German Novelle of Poetic Realism. 1954. Third printing, 1962. Pp. xiv, 168. Paper $ 4.00.
12. Percy Matenko. LUDWIG TIECK AND AMERICA. 1954. Out of print.
13. Wilhelm Dilthey. THE ESSENCE OF PHILOSOPHY. Rendered into English by Stephen A. Emery and William T. Emery. 1954, 1961. Pp. xii, 78. Paper $ 1.50.
14. Edwin H. Zeydel and B. Q. Morgan. GREGORIUS. A Medieval Oedipus Legend by Hartmann von Aue. Translated in Rhyming Couplets with Introduction and Notes. 1955. Out of print.
15. Alfred G. Steer, Jr. GOETHE'S SOCIAL PHILOSOPHY AS REVEALED IN CAMPAGNE IN FRANKREICH AND BELAGERUNG VON MAINZ, With three full-page illustrations. 1955. Pp. xiv, 178. Paper $ 4.00.
16. Edwin H. Zeydel. GOETHE THE LYRIST. 100 Poems in New Translations facing the Original Texts. With a Biographical Introduction and an Appendix on Musical Settings. 1955. Pp. xviii, 182. 2nd ed. 1958. 3rd ed. 1965. Cloth $ 4.00.
17. Hermann J. Weigand. THREE CHAPTERS ON COURTLY LOVE IN ARTHURIAN FRANCE AND GERMANY. Out of print.
18. George Fenwick Jones. WITTENWILER'S „RING" AND THE ANONYMOUS SCOTS POEM „COLKELBIE SOW". Two Comic-Didactic Works from the Fifteenth Century. Translated into English. With five illustrations. 1956. Pp. xiv, 246. Paper $ 4.50.
19. George C. Schoolfield. THE FIGURE OF THE MUSICIAN IN GERMAN LITERATURE. 1956. Out of print.
20. Edwin H. Zeydel. POEMS OF GOETHE. A Sequel to GOETHE THE LYRIST. New Translations facing the Originals. With an Introduction and a List of Musical Settings. 1957. Pp. xii, 126. Paper $ 3.25. Out of print.
21. Joseph Mileck. HERMANN HESSE AND HIS CRITICS. The Criticism and Bibliography of Half a Century. 1958. Out of print.
22. Ernest N. Kirrmann. DEATH AND THE PLOWMAN or THE BOHEMIAN PLOWMAN. A Disputatious and Consolatory Dialogue about Death from the Year 1400. Translated from the Modern German Version of Alois Bernt. 1958. Pp. xviii, 40. Paper $ 1.85.
23. Edwin H. Zeydel. RUODLIEB, THE EARLIEST COURTLY NOVEL (after 1050). Introduction, Text, Translation, Commentary, and Textual Notes. With seven illustrations. 1959, Second printing, 1963. Pp. xii, 165. Paper $ 4.50.
24. John T. Krumpelmann. THE MAIDEN OF ORLEANS. A Romantic Tragedy in Five Acts by Friedrich Schiller. Translated into English in the Verse Forms of the Original German. 1959. Out print.
25. George Fenwick Jones. HONOR IN GERMAN LITERATURE. 1959. Pp. xii, 208. Paper $ 4.50.
26. MIDDLE AGES—REFORMATION—VOLKSKUNDE. FESTSCHRIFT for John G. Kunstmann Twenty Essays. 1959. Out of print.
27. Martin Dyck. NOVALIS AND MATHEMATICS. 1960. Pp. xii, 109. Paper $ 3.50.
28. Claude Hill and Ralph Ley. THE DRAMA OF GERMAN EXPRESSIONISM. A German-English Bibliography. 1960. Pp. xii, 211. Out of print.
29. George C. Schoolfield. THE GERMAN LYRIC OF THE BAROQUE IN ENGLISH TRANSLATION. 1961. Pp. x, 380. Paper $ 7.00.
30. John Fitzell. THE HERMIT IN GERMAN LITERATURE. (From Lessing to Eichendorff.) 1961. Pp. xiv, 130. Paper $ 4.50.
31. Heinrich von Kleist. THE BROKEN PITCHER. A Comedy. Translated into English Verse by B. Q. Morgan. 1961. Out of print.